Using Self-Assessment to Improve Student Learning

Using Self-Assessment to Improve Student Learning synthesizes research on self-assessment and translates it into actionable guidelines and principles for pre-service and in-service teachers and for school leaders, teacher educators, and researchers. Situated beyond the simple how-to frameworks currently available for teachers and graduate students, this volume illuminates self-assessment's complexities and substantial promise to strategically move students toward self-regulated learning and internalized goals. Addressing theory, empirical evidence, and common implementation issues, the book's developmental approach to quality self-assessment practices will help teachers, leaders, and scholars maximize their influence on student self-regulation and learning.

Lois Ruth Harris is Senior Lecturer in the School of Education and the Arts at Central Queensland University and Senior Research Fellow at the Learning Sciences Institute Australia at Australian Catholic University.

Gavin T. L. Brown is Professor, Associate Dean Post-Graduate, and Director of the Quantitative Data Analysis and Research Unit in the Faculty of Education and Social Work at the University of Auckland, New Zealand.

Student Assessment for Educators
Edited by James H. McMillan,
Virginia Commonwealth University, USA

Using Self-Assessment to Improve Student Learning
Lois Ruth Harris and Gavin T. L. Brown

Using Feedback to Improve Learning
Maria Araceli Ruiz-Primo and Susan M. Brookhart

**Using Formative Assessment to Enhance Learning,
Achievement, and Academic Self-Regulation**
Heidi L. Andrade and Margaret Heritage

**Using Students' Assessment Mistakes and Learning
Deficits to Enhance Motivation and Learning**
James H. McMillan

Using Self-Assessment to Improve Student Learning

Lois Ruth Harris
and
Gavin T. L. Brown

Routledge
Taylor & Francis Group

NEW YORK AND LONDON

First published 2018
by Routledge
711 Third Avenue, New York, NY 10017

and by Routledge
2 Park Square, Milton Park, Abingdon, Oxon, OX14 4RN

Routledge is an imprint of the Taylor & Francis Group, an informa business

Library of Congress Cataloging-in-Publication Data
A catalog record for this book has been requested

ISBN: 978-1-138-28336-7 (hbk)
ISBN: 978-1-138-28337-4 (pbk)
ISBN: 978-1-351-03697-9 (ebk)

Typeset in Sabon
by Apex CoVantage, LLC

Contents

Preface

Like it or not, students are already self-assessing within your classroom. During our classroom teaching days, both of us witnessed plenty of examples of unprompted student self-assessment, Lois in Australia and the United States and Gavin in New Zealand. Such self-assessment was evidenced in student comments like *"I'm no good at this"* when asked to persist with a task, *"But I worked really hard"* when protesting a low grade, and *"You added up my marks wrong"* in reaction to potentially inaccurate scoring. Chances are you've heard your own students say these lines or something similar.

Statements like this are clear evidence that regardless of teacher actions or students' actual ability, students self-assess. They use information available to them to decide how good they are at something or if their performance is or is not competent. They may draw on many sources of information: external feedback like grades, their own observations, or something said or written by a parent or peer. The judgment may also be virtually groundless, just a hunch or intuition; they may be unaware of or unable to understand the external criteria or standards that were actually used to judge their work.

However, self-assessments that lead to self-beliefs can have serious educational implications. Students may choose to quit trying on a task or to avoid subjects within a domain in which they believe they lack ability or competence. Such decisions could be crippling for the life chances of a learner. The reverse can also be dangerous. Imagine a student who believes he or she is competent but who actually requires significant improvement. Instead of working hard on weaknesses, such a student is unlikely to be successful, as he or she probably won't invest sufficient effort of the right type. Cinematic representations of driver's education in American high schools provide good examples of this phenomenon. Being overconfident or ignoring important feedback about needs by discounting the source of the information (e.g., *Boring old fuddy-duddy driving instructors who want to take away my fun or freedom*) results in dangerous driving.

Although self-assessment in some form always occurs naturally, beneficial forms of self-assessment are a learned behavior. If students have not been taught how to self-assess, their evaluations often tend to be very global. For example, many of the students who have told us they were "no good at English" may have struggled with particular aspects of the domain (e.g., spelling, written grammar, text structure) but were not poor at all aspects. Some were voracious readers. Others could memorize and perform their favorite music lyrics with emotion and energy or come up with extremely creative and insightful ideas when writing. However, they usually took one aspect of the domain (e.g., proficiency at written English spelling and grammar) and applied it to the whole.

Students who have not been taught how to realistically self-assess may also measure their work against unrealistic standards. Lois's oldest son, who is five, began school this year, entering what we call the prep year here in Australia (referred to as kindergarten in the United States, reception in the United Kingdom, and year 1 in New Zealand). Soon afterward, he came home and stated that he was terrible at handwriting. He had spent time looking at the perfectly drawn model letters on the classroom walls and activity sheets and, rather than seeing them as something he could aspire to achieve over time, thought they were an immediate target to be reached. Nobody had told him he was "bad" at writing; he had just observed his own letter formation against the model and found it lacking. For several months thereafter, he lacked the motivation to try to improve. He would say, "It's no use" when asked to practice at home. In an era when perfection is praised and mistakes are discouraged (McMillan, 2018), it is easy to see why students may come to false and global assumptions about their capabilities and how these have the potential to decrease motivation and effort. Simultaneously, their self-assessments usually fail to provide any kind of feedback that could help them actually improve.

Ultimately, the power of self-assessment, when implemented well, is that students will (a) gain a much better and more nuanced understanding of what quality work and performance is within a domain, (b) understand more accurately how their work compares with external standards, (c) receive timely feedback on their work in language they understand, and (d) use this feedback within a cycle of self-regulated learning toward improved outcomes. Empowering students to take steps to identify and improve weaknesses in their work can also increase their motivation and agency as learners.

However, the promise of self-assessment has to be tempered with a realistic appraisal of human nature. Humans have identity, well-being, and ego that can be threatened when "failure" becomes apparent. Becoming aware of one's own performance or task deficiencies can be threatening to the self. People may welcome such knowledge, become defensive, or even aggressively attack the perceived source of the information. However, unless weakness is identified, it cannot be addressed (at least that is the fundamental principle of the scientific method). Thus, there is a tension each individual must negotiate around how ego and sense of well-being are handled when deficiencies are identified and acknowledged (Boekaerts & Niemivirta, 2000).

A further problem for self-assessment is identified when closely examining the term itself, the question of who or what is actually being assessed. In educational self-assessment, we are not asking for an evaluation of the self (Kasanen & Räty, 2002) but rather of the self's work. However, for many, it is difficult to separate "my work" from "myself," and our previous work has clearly demonstrated that this problem exists for many school-children (Andrade & Brown, 2016; Brown & Harris, 2013; Harris & Brown, 2013). Children care about how they appear to themselves, their peers, their teachers, and their parents. Thus, no matter how much potential academic benefit self-assessment can bring, it takes strength of will to engage meaningfully with feedback that identifies shortcomings in our work.

In our teaching practice and research, we have found self-assessment to be a very powerful tool but one that is not always easy to implement in the classroom. Although students naturally judge their own work in some way or another, quality self-assessment in the classroom requires students to draw on external criteria and standards for what constitutes quality work and then use these to evaluate their current capabilities and identify areas for improvement. Drawing on Douglas Adams's *Hitchhiker's Guide to the Galaxy* series, student self-assessment is not a matter of entering the Total Perspective Vortex in which Zaphod Beeblebrox discovered that he really was the most important person in the universe (Adams, 1995). The process of setting aside your own personal criteria and instead evaluating work using socially accepted criteria is not necessarily intuitive for students. Self-assessment often takes place in a classroom setting, which is a complex social space. Additionally, students have to be able to learn how to formulate effective feedback to themselves and be given the time and space to implement changes.

This book draws on our own classroom experiences, alongside research from around the world, to help you (whether you are a teacher, school leader, teacher educator, or emerging researcher) to understand the complexities of classroom self-assessment. These insights will allow you to guide students and prospective teachers to effectively participate in self-assessment within your own educational spaces. It will help you define self-assessment and gain a deep understanding of the theories of self-regulation and formative assessment that underpin the use of self-assessment in classroom contexts. Additionally, it will highlight common problems and challenges with implementation and identify strengths and weaknesses associated with many

common self-assessment practices. The book concludes by sharing suggested steps we consider teachers should take when planning and implementing self-assessment. We also provide some
guidance to school leaders about how to implement self-assessment
within schools.

Before you begin, we'd like to point out a few conventions
within the book. We've made an effort to highlight student
voices within this volume because ultimately, within the classroom, they are the actual self-assessors. Hence, we have chosen to italicize quotes from student participants in our own and
colleagues' studies, alongside other statements from the student
perspective, in order to draw attention to these voices. Also,
given that school systems all have different starting ages, school
years, and ways of naming particular cohort levels, we have
chosen to retain the terminology used in the original studies
rather than attempt to convert these descriptors to American
grade levels.

We hope this book will help you better understand and appreciate the complexities of enacting self-assessment with students
while simultaneously empowering you to use this valuable practice within your own schools and classrooms!

References

Adams, D. (1995). *The restaurant at the end of the universe*. New York,
NY: Del Rey.

Andrade, H. L., & Brown, G. T. L. (2016). Student self-assessment in
the classroom. In G. T. L. Brown & L. R. Harris (Eds.), *Handbook
of human and social conditions in assessment* (pp. 319–334). New
York, NY: Routledge.

Boekaerts, M., & Niemivirta, M. (2000). Self-regulated learning: Finding a balance between learning goals and ego-protective goals. In M.
Boekaerts, P. R. Pintrich, & M. Zeidner (Eds.), *Handbook of self-
regulation* (pp. 417–450). San Diego, CA: Academic Press.

Brown, G. T. L., & Harris, L. R. (2013). Student self-assessment.
In J. H. McMillan (Ed.), *Sage handbook of research on classroom
assessment* (pp. 367–393). Thousand Oaks, CA: Sage.

Harris, L. R., & Brown, G. T. L. (2013). Opportunities and obstacles
to consider when using peer- and self-assessment to improve student

learning: Case studies into teachers' implementation. *Teaching and Teacher Education*, 36, 101–111. doi:10.1016/j.tate.2013.07.008

Kasanen, K., & Räty, H. (2002). "You be sure now to be honest in your assessment": Teaching and learning self-assessment. *Social Psychology of Education*, 5(4), 313–328. doi:10.1023/A:1020993427849

McMillan, J. H. (2018). *Using students' assessment mistakes and learning deficits to enhance motivation and learning*. New York, NY: Routledge.

Acknowledgments

As with any major project, a book is always a team effort, and there are many people who deserve thanks for their contributions, help, and support during this work. We'd like to start by thanking the series editor, Jim McMillan, both for inviting us to write this book in the first place and for his encouraging and thoughtful editorial comments on the draft manuscript. We'd also like to thank the Routledge team, particularly Daniel Schwartz, for their help throughout all aspects of the publication process.

We would also like to acknowledge the support of colleagues from the University of Auckland, Central Queensland University, and other institutions who have listened to our ideas and provided us with lively debate about this topic. Particular thanks go to Heidi Andrade, Ernesto Panadero, and Anna Fletcher, all of whom have given us permission to share examples of quality real-world self-assessment practices from their respective studies within this book and have provided feedback on some of our ideas. We would also like to acknowledge the teacher and student participants in our own and colleagues' studies who have contributed to our knowledge of quality self-assessment practice. Thanks are due to teachers Maria Comba and Angela Fremont, whose rubrics from the Arts Achieve project are shared within this book.

Lastly, it is important to recognize the love and support from our respective families who have been long suffering as we have put this manuscript together. Lois's husband, Chris, and her three small children, Alexander, Rebecca, and James, have been supportive, even when they may have had other ideas about how mum could be spending her time. Lois's sister, Mary, was kind enough to help improve the diagrams, proofread the final manuscript, and compile the index, and her parents and in-laws provided some much-needed childcare as she finished the final draft. Gavin's patience when life at times slowed manuscript progress was greatly appreciated, as were his thoughtful ideas and revisions. It is always fun to have you as a coauthor.

Gavin would like to acknowledge the continuing love and life support offered by his amazing wife, Judith. Sure, he thinks the big ideas, but she figures out what he wears, eats, and so on. He has had the pleasure of working with Lois since her postdoctoral research fellowship at the University of Auckland (2008–2009). We sharpen each other's thinking, writing, and research. Thanks goes to Lois for leading another great team project.

We hope you enjoy this book and make use of our ideas. We would love to hear about your own classroom self-assessment implementations that work (or don't work), as this information will help further hone and shape our ideas about quality practice.

1

Introduction
Why Use Self-Assessment in the Classroom?

Research makes it abundantly clear that although people conduct automatic self-evaluations, it is very difficult for them to realistically self-assess their competence, especially while they are still learning complex skills (e.g., composition, mathematical analysis) (Brown & Harris, 2013; Dunning, Heath, & Suls, 2004). Additionally, within school contexts, there are often quite specific criteria and standards around what constitutes a quality or competent performance. These tend to be determined by external authorities (e.g., departments or ministries of education). Students have to understand these external criteria if they are to demonstrate their learning in the ways valued by the education system, school, and/or classroom teacher.

It is not just novices and the less competent who easily misjudge the quality of their own work. Very good students may often unrealistically underestimate their capabilities (Brown & Harris, 2013), and an inaccurate negative self-assessment can be the basis for detrimental decisions (e.g., giving up on learning a difficult skill, even though appropriate progress is being made, because the learner is dissatisfied with how long it is taking to develop the skill) (Butler, 2011).

Conversely, many people have strong tendencies to unrealistically *overestimate* how good their work is (Dunning et al., 2004). It is hard to discern and admit that one's work is below average or substandard. Additionally, it is difficult to accept and understand external or socially mandated criteria. It is much easier to use personal criteria (e.g., *I tried hard, so it must be good*), but these are seldom well aligned with externally accepted standards. Thus, without constructive feedback and effective instruction, students are likely to misjudge the quality of their own work in the classroom, particularly if they are less-proficient or novice learners. Learning to self-assess realistically is a competence that students have to acquire, in addition to the skills, abilities, or knowledge intended by the curriculum (Brown & Harris, 2014).

Getting students to effectively self-assess within the classroom is more than just helping them form opinions about their own work. It is about

1. guiding students to a deep understanding of appropriate standards for judging the quality of work;
2. helping them understand how to evaluate their performance against those standards;
3. assisting them to arrive at a realistic understanding of their performance or work; and
4. teaching them to interpret and use these data in ways that will benefit their learning.

This means that teachers must help students overcome any natural ego-protective or self-deprecating tendencies they may have so that they can realistically identify what they need to work on to improve.

Although classroom self-assessment participation is normally low-stakes (i.e., no or weak consequences), it is important to understand that even under these conditions, self-assessment can have potentially serious consequences for students. Inaccurate perceptions of their work and abilities can lead students to make decisions that limit their options (e.g., avoiding certain subjects despite having capability) or undermine their achievement (e.g., not studying enough because they falsely believe they are competent) (Dunlosky & Rawson, 2012; Ramdass & Zimmerman, 2008). Students, especially those with perfectionist mind-sets, may not want to identify and acknowledge potential shortcomings in their work. In a classroom situation where self-assessments are shared with teachers or even peers, participation in self-assessment can place students in situations where they feel uncomfortable, as they may fear the judgment or negative evaluations of their teacher or peers (Harris & Brown, 2013; Raider-Roth, 2005).

Why Self-Assessment Is Vital Within the Classroom

The power of self-assessment is that it is a process that occurs internally within the student (Brookhart, 2016), as the student knows most about what was intended. It is highly likely that coming to conclusions for and by oneself about the quality of one's own work will have a strong positive effect on learning progress. Feedback the student generates is going to be understood and is likely to be acted on by that person. Furthermore, the self is always available to an individual, so "dollops of feedback," as Hattie (1999) put it, are continually accessible. If student self-assessment can be aligned with curricular criteria and standards, then it not only gives students more agency and independence within the learning environment but also can potentially allow them to accelerate their progress, as they no longer will have to wait for feedback from the teacher to devise their next learning steps. Despite the potential risks and challenges associated with self-assessment, discussed extensively in Chapter 3, there are two fundamental reasons why teachers ought to actively promote and structure self-assessment within classrooms. First, it is an integral part of self-regulated learning. Second, without the proper guidance and training, students' evaluations are highly varied and may align poorly with the external standards of the curriculum.

Although there are multiple models of self-regulation (Panadero, 2017), all models draw attention to the importance of the individual's conscious, motivated, and aware engagement in learning strategies (e.g., memorization, mind mapping), environmental control (e.g., planned study times without distractions), and cognitive control (e.g., monitoring strategic effectiveness, maintaining positive motivation) (Dinsmore & Wilson, 2016). Self-regulation of learning requires students to be consciously aware of what they are doing and whether the work meets personal and environmental expectations. Students must have a realistic appreciation of their own strengths (so they can be built on) and weaknesses (so they can be worked on) (Boekaerts, 1997; Pintrich, 1995; Zimmerman, 2008). Self-assessment is clearly a vital part of self-regulation, as it allows the student to draw on important metacognitive competencies (e.g., self-observation, self-judgment, self-reaction, task analysis, self-motivation, and self-control) (Zimmerman, 2002). Thus, as Brookhart (2016) explains,

> One of the main functions of self-assessment is to engage students at a deep level with their learning goals and the criteria for success, a foundational principle in formative assessment. That is, what is effective about self-assessment is that it fosters student engagement with the formative assessment cycle (i.e., Where am I going? Where am I now? Where to next?), giving students a tool for self-regulation of learning (setting goals, monitoring, adjusting, and reflecting).
>
> (p. 361)

Brookhart (2016) and other researchers (e.g., Andrade & Brookhart, 2016; Andrade & Heritage, 2018) have noted the strong similarities between formative assessment's goals and processes and those that are thought to underpin self-regulated learning. These help explain why self-assessment is considered a key strategy within both formative assessment and self-regulated learning. Participating in classroom self-assessment has been shown to help develop self-regulation skills (i.e., set targets, evaluate progress relative to target criteria, and improve the quality of their learning outcomes) (Andrade, Du, & Wang, 2008;

Andrade, Du, & Mycek, 2010; Brookhart, Andolina, Zuza, & Furman, 2004; Fletcher, 2016). Additionally, it is associated with improved motivation, engagement, and efficacy (Fletcher, 2016; Griffiths & Davies, 1993; Klenowski, 1995; Munns & Woodward, 2006; Panadero, Jonsson, & Botella, 2017; Schunk, 1996), reducing dependence on the teacher (Sadler, 1989).

However, student involvement in assessment is not consistently connected to greater self-regulation (Dinsmore & Wilson, 2016). Unguided evaluations of the self's actions or work are often highly personal and variable, so it is logical that within the classroom they would only sometimes be consistent with the curriculum standards and expectations meant to guide learning. Students within the classroom will often have vastly different ideas about what should count (e.g., accuracy, creativity, effort) and what an acceptable standard of work may look like. As Eva and Regehr (2011) note, "Increasingly it is being recognized that self-assessment as a process of personal reflection based on an unguided review of practice and experience . . . is inherently flawed" (p. 312).

The challenge is that within a school context, the criteria and standards for successful academic performance are external to the student, embedded in each society's curriculum documents and teaching practices. Students have to learn to evaluate their performance against the objectives or standards specified within each curriculum area rather than against their own intuitive notions as to what is acceptable or good. Learners often need help to develop realistic self-awareness and to engage with the quality characteristics of work within the domains they are studying. Although what students value in their own work does matter (e.g., it is important to know if they think their work is good because they worked hard on it), students must also be taught the rules and standards by which their work will be evaluated by others. Hence, teachers need to teach not only the curriculum but also the skill of assessing work against relevant external standards (Brown & Harris, 2014).

In conclusion, the challenge with self-assessment in schools occurs not because learners are unable to self-assess but because they need specific scaffolding and support from their teacher to use this process effectively in relation to societal expectations embedded in the curriculum. However self-assessment is understood (and it can be defined in multiple ways; Panadero, Brown, & Strijbos, 2016), its most powerful promise is the expectation that engaging in the process will raise student academic performance. This happens because self-assessment requires pupils to self-regulate and consequently improve their learning relative to the goals and standards of schooling (Andrade, 2010; Black & Wiliam, 1998a; Butler & Winne, 1995; Hattie & Timperley, 2007; Ramdass & Zimmerman, 2008).

The goal of the rest of this book is to lay out theories, strategies, and methods of self-assessment that are likely to contribute to greater self-regulation of learning as well as greater learning itself. We hope to provide a framework that teachers, school leaders, and teacher educators can use to ensure students learn to judge their work realistically in relation to curriculum-based standards. This book will assist you in supporting your students to effectively self-assess by helping them develop skills in making realistic judgments about the strengths and weaknesses of their own work. The long-term goal is that even after their time at school is over, students will continue to engage in thoughtful assessment and evaluation of their work as an essential competence of successful adult life. Additionally, because school self-assessment takes place within the social and psychological complexity of the classroom environment, this book will alert you to common problems that threaten the validity and utility of self-assessment.

Defining Self-Assessment Within Educational Settings

Many diverse terms, including *self-assessment, self-evaluation, self-reflection, self-monitoring,* and more generally, *reflection,* are used to describe the process of students assessing and providing feedback on their own work. Within academic settings, such processes as self-grading, self-testing, and self-rating also require students to assess their own performance. Hence, "self-assessment is a descriptive and evaluative act carried out by the student concerning his or her own work and academic abilities" (Brown & Harris, 2013, p. 368).

Under this broad definition, diverse practices can be considered as self-assessment (although all are not equally valuable in relation to learning, something discussed in more detail in Chapter 4 when particular practices are explored). We must point out, though, that this definition is not uncontested; there are many experts who argue that the term *self-assessment* should be used only when qualitative judgments are made in relation to criteria and standards as opposed to the simpler act of scoring or marking one's own work (e.g., Andrade, 2010, in press; Andrade & Valtcheva, 2009; Panadero, 2011). These researchers argue that quantitative self-evaluations of performance (e.g., students' predictions of how many questions they will answer correctly or marking their own test papers) do not require students to undertake much, if any, reflection about the quality of their work. Additionally, such exercises do not necessarily lead students to generate feedback, which Andrade (in press) argues is the ultimate point of self-assessment.

Although we agree that such qualitative self-assessment practices are more powerful for learning (Brown & Harris, 2013), we take the stance that initially students may not have sufficient content expertise to engage in more complex and rewarding forms of self-assessment. We have argued that a curriculum is needed to support students to become proficient at realistic self-assessment of their work while progressively developing their ability to make more sophisticated judgments about work quality (Brown & Harris, 2014). Hence, despite their simplicity, self-rating and self-scoring practices may be a useful starting point for children who are just beginning to evaluate their own work relative to external standards and who need to learn to judge their work in a manner similar to teachers (Brown & Harris, 2014).

For example, a student's first experience with self-assessment might legitimately be a very simple self-scoring or self-marking assessment, such as scoring one's own work when correct objective answers have been provided (e.g., the common practice of getting primary schoolchildren to correct their own work on simple arithmetic quizzes or spelling tests). Students may also predict how well they think they will do on a forthcoming task (i.e., prospective judgment of learning; Dunlosky & Rawson, 2012), or they could be asked to retrospectively evaluate their current level of understanding (Baars, Vink, van Gog, de Bruin, & Paas, 2014). For example, the Traffic Lights classroom strategy is a retrospective self-assessment activity where students display to the teacher a red, yellow, or green color to signal, respectively, a low, medium, or high level of understanding (Black, Harrison, Lee, Marshall, & Wiliam, 2003). As student self-assessment and domain abilities progress, they will have greater competence in judging the strengths and weaknesses of their own work in light of the often quite abstract criteria and standards embedded in a rubric (Panadero & Jonsson, 2013).

Although these are all quite different forms of self-assessment, what distinguishes these from other assessment practices is that the student carries them out. Hence, we have argued that

> self-assessment takes place when students impute or infer that their work or their ability to do that work has some sort of quality characteristics, and this self-assessment may, in its most simple form, be a quantity estimate (i.e., How many task requirements have I satisfied?) or a quality estimate (i.e., How well have I done?).
>
> (Brown & Harris, 2013, p. 368)

Clearly, different self-assessment processes and approaches may be appropriate for differing ages and stages of development, an issue we will explore more thoroughly in Chapter 4.

Panadero and Alonso-Tapia (2013) also highlight the important distinction between "self-assessment as a learning strategy that a student can activate" and "self-assessment as a pedagogical strategy through which the teacher asks the students to reflect on their work" (p. 554). They argue that both theoretical perspectives must be integrated if self-assessment is to have a maximum effect on learning. Although it may be reasonable to assume that adults can independently monitor their academic or professional performance against appropriate community or personal standards (Bourke, 2016; Tan, 2008), within schools, teachers are expected to initiate and support student self-assessment activities. Good pedagogical practice will support realistic self-assessment and has to include explicitly teaching students how, when, and why to self-assess. This includes helping students to become realistic in their self-assessments and to use that information as a guide for further learning. There are many ways this may occur (e.g., by a teacher's direct instruction, through having peers explain the reasons and processes they used in reaching a judgment about their own work, via student opportunities to practice; Panadero & Alonso-Tapia, 2013). Teachers should take an active role in setting up situations where students learn how to self-assess and can practice self-assessment. It is through practice, with feedback from trusted teachers, peers, and/or parents, that students will learn how to better self-regulate their learning and their self-assessments.

Another challenge for self-assessment is associated with the term *assessment*. This label suggests that there is equivalence to other evaluative techniques, such as tests. However, as this book will show, the accuracy and consistency (i.e., validity and reliability) of self-assessments is highly influenced by construct-irrelevant factors (e.g., ego enhancement, self-effacement, lack of psychological safety). Thus, we conclude that self-assessment in most educational settings is an extremely useful pedagogical practice and a valuable life skill but a very poor measurement or estimate of actual competence. As written elsewhere, we conclude that

> self-assessments should not count toward grades, and perhaps, should be private. . . . Perhaps, consistent with our other work (Andrade, 2010; Brown & Harris, 2014), any attempt to treat student self-assessment as a formal assessment should be eschewed, given the social and psychological reasons for over- or underestimation.
>
> (Andrade & Brown, 2016, p. 327)

Clearly, self-assessment is a complex practice to implement successfully in the classroom. As such, before doing so, it is critical that the teacher considers how self-assessment can be integrated as a key process throughout any learning activity. At the same time, students need to come to an understanding of their roles as agents within the learning and evaluation process and develop a commitment to and the courage for realism in their self-assessments. A useful framework for guiding self-assessment in learning is to use three key feedback questions (Hattie & Timperley, 2007, p. 86):

- Where am I going? (What are the goals?)
- How am I going? (What progress is being made toward the goal?)
- Where to next? (What activities need to be undertaken to make better progress?)

Regardless of how self-assessment is defined, it must be implemented in ways that provide learners with helpful feedback if it is to positively influence learning.

Further Exploration of Self-Assessment Within the Classroom

This chapter has helped define self-assessment and explain why it is a valuable strategy to teach to your students. Not only is it helpful as students develop agency within learning and assessment processes, encouraging them to engage in a process of self-regulated learning, but it is also powerful because it allows learners to generate just-in-time formative feedback that can lead to improvement. This chapter also provides a broad definition of self-assessment, identifying a range of practices that can be subsumed under this banner.

Subsequent chapters in this book will help you unpack the theory underpinning classroom self-assessment and relate it to practice, assisting you to improve the use of this important tool with your own students. Chapter 2 will situate self-assessment within self-regulation and formative assessment theories to understand why and how self-assessment benefit is maximized. However, implementing classroom self-assessment is not without potential difficulties. Chapter 3 explores common challenges teachers may encounter when executing self-assessment, focusing on some of the specific threats to the validity and realism of self-assessment that must be mitigated. This chapter identifies these challenges and provides advice on how to manage them within the classroom. Chapter 4 will then examine some popular forms of self-assessment, highlighting the strengths and weaknesses associated with each approach and identifying particular contexts where each are most useful. The final chapter of the book brings together key recommendations around how to successfully implement self-assessment within the classroom, along with ideas on how you might go about implementing a school- or department-wide approach to self-assessment.

References

Andrade, H. L. (2010). Students as the definitive source of formative assessment: Academic self-assessment and the self-regulation of learning. In H. L. Andrade & G. J. Cizek (Eds.), *Handbook of formative assessment* (pp. 90–105). New York, NY: Routledge.

Andrade, H. L. (in press). Feedback in the context of self-assessment. In A. Lipnevich & J. K. Smith (Eds.), *The Cambridge handbook of instructional feedback*. Cambridge, England: Cambridge University Press.

Andrade, H. L., & Brookhart, S. M. (2016). The role of classroom assessment in supporting self-regulated learning. In D. Laveault & L. Allal (Eds.), *Assessment for learning: Meeting the challenge of implementation* (pp. 293–309). Cham, Switzerland: Springer International.

Andrade, H. L., & Brown, G. T. L. (2016). Student self-assessment in the classroom. In G. T. L. Brown & L. R. Harris (Eds.), *Handbook of human and social conditions in assessment* (pp. 319–334). New York, NY: Routledge.

Andrade, H. L., Du, Y., & Mycek, K. (2010). Rubric-referenced self-assessment and middle school students' writing. *Assessment in Education: Principles, Policy & Practice, 17*(2), 199–214. doi:10.1080/09695941003696172

Andrade, H. L., Du, Y., & Wang, X. (2008). Putting rubrics to the test: The effect of a model, criteria generation, and rubric-referenced self-assessment on elementary school students' writing. *Educational Measurement: Issues and Practice, 27*(2), 3–13. doi:10.1111/j.1745-3992.2008.00118.x

Andrade, H. L., & Heritage, M. (2018). *Using formative assessment to enhance learning, achievement, and academic self-regulation.* New York, NY: Routledge.

Andrade, H. L., & Valtcheva, A. (2009). Promoting learning and achievement through self-assessment. *Theory into Practice, 28*(1), 12–19.

Baars, M., Vink, S., van Gog, T., de Bruin, A., & Paas, F. (2014). Effects of training self-assessment and using assessment standards on retrospective and prospective monitoring of problem solving. *Learning & Instruction, 33*, 92–107. doi:10.1016/j.learninstruc.2014.04.004

Black, P., Harrison, C., Lee, C., Marshall, B., & Wiliam, D. (2003). *Assessment for learning: Putting it into practice.* Maidenhead, England: Open University Press.

Black, P., & Wiliam, D. (1998a). Assessment and classroom learning. *Assessment in Education, 5*(1), 7–74.

Boekaerts, M. (1997). Self-regulated learning: A new concept embraced by researchers, policy makers, educators, teachers, and students. *Learning and Instruction, 7*, 161–186.

Bourke, R. (2016). Liberating the learner through self-assessment. *Cambridge Journal of Education, 46*(1), 97–111. doi:10.1080/0305764X.2015.1015963

Brookhart, S. M. (2016). Building assessments that work in the classroom. In G. T. L. Brown & L. R. Harris (Eds.), *Handbook of human and social conditions in assessment* (pp. 351–365). New York, NY: Routledge.

Brookhart, S. M., Andolina, M., Zuza, M., & Furman, R. (2004). Minute math: An action research study of student self-assessment. *Educational Studies in Mathematics, 57*, 213–227.

Brown, G. T. L., & Harris, L. R. (2013). Student self-assessment. In J. H. McMillan (Ed.), *Sage handbook of research on classroom assessment* (pp. 367–393). Thousand Oaks, CA: Sage.

Brown, G. T. L., & Harris, L. R. (2014). The future of self-assessment in classroom practice: Reframing self-assessment as a core competency. *Frontline Learning Research, 3*, 22–30. doi:10.14786/flr.v2i1.24

Butler, D. L., & Winne, P. H. (1995). Feedback and self-regulated learning: A theoretical synthesis. *Review of Educational Research, 65*(3), 245–281.

Butler, R. (2011). Are positive illusions about academic competence always adaptive, under all circumstances: New results and future directions. *International Journal of Educational Research, 50*(4), 251–256. doi:10.1016/j.ijer.2011.08.006

Dinsmore, D. L., & Wilson, H. E. (2016). Student participation in assessment: Does it influence self-regulation? In G. T. L. Brown &

L. R. Harris (Eds.), *Handbook of human and social conditions in assessment* (pp. 145–168). New York, NY: Routledge.

Dunlosky, J., & Rawson, K. A. (2012). Overconfidence produces underachievement: Inaccurate self-evaluations undermine students' learning and retention. *Learning & Instruction, 22*(4), 271–280. doi:10.1016/j.learninstruc.2011.08.003

Dunning, D., Heath, C., & Suls, J. M. (2004). Flawed self-assessment: Implications for health, education, and the workplace. *Psychological Science in the Public Interest, 5*(3), 69–106.

Eva, K. W., & Regehr, G. (2011). Exploring the divergence between self-assessment and self-monitoring. *Advances in Health Sciences Education, 16(3)*, 311–329. doi:10.1007/s10459-010-9263-2

Fletcher, A. K. (2016). Exceeding expectations: Scaffolding agentic engagement through assessment as learning. *Educational Research, 58*(4), 400–419. doi:10.1080/00131881.2016.1235909

Griffiths, M., & Davies, C. (1993). Learning to learn: Action research from an equal opportunities perspective in a junior school. *British Educational Research Journal, 19*(1), 43–58.

Harris, L. R., & Brown, G. T. L. (2013). Opportunities and obstacles to consider when using peer- and self-assessment to improve student learning: Case studies into teachers' implementation. *Teaching and Teacher Education, 36*, 101–111. doi:10.1016/j.tate.2013.07.008

Hattie, J. A. (1999, August). *Influences on student learning.* Paper presented at the Inaugural Lecture: Professor of Education, University of Auckland, New Zealand.

Hattie, J. A., & Timperley, H. (2007). The power of feedback. *Review of Educational Research, 77*(1), 81–112.

Klenowski, V. (1995). Student self-evaluation processes in student-centered teaching and learning contexts of Australia and England. *Assessment in Education: Principles, Policy & Practice, 2*(2), 145–163. doi:10.1080/0969594950020203

Munns, G., & Woodward, H. (2006). Student engagement and student self-assessment: The REAL framework. *Assessment in Education: Principles, Policy and Practice, 13*(2), 193–213.

Panadero, E. (2011). *Instructional help for self-assessment and self-regulation: Evaluation of the efficacy of self-assessment scripts vs. rubrics* (Doctoral dissertation). Universidad Autónoma de Madrid, Spain.

Panadero, E. (2017). A review of self-regulated learning: Six models and four directions for research. *Frontiers in Psychology, 8*, 1–28. doi:10.3389/fpsyg.2017.00422

Panadero, E., & Alonso-Tapia, J. (2013). Self-assessment: Theoretical and practical connotations: When it happens, how is it acquired and what to do to develop it in our students. *Electronic Journal of Research in Educational Psychology, 11*(2), 551–576.

Panadero, E., Brown, G. L., & Strijbos, J.-W. (2016). The future of student self-assessment: A review of known unknowns and potential directions. *Educational Psychology Review, 28*(4), 803–830. doi:10.1007/s10648-015-9350-2

Panadero, E., & Jonsson, A. (2013). The use of scoring rubrics for formative assessment purposes revisited: A review. *Educational Research Review, 9*, 129–144. doi:10.1016/j.edurev.2013.01.002

Panadero, E., Jonsson, A., & Botella, J. (2017). Effects of self-assessment on self-regulated learning and self-efficacy: Four meta-analyses. *Educational Research Review, 22*(Supplement C), 74–98. doi:10.1016/j.edurev.2017.08.004

Pintrich, P. R. (1995). *Understanding self-regulated learning.* San Francisco, CA: Jossey-Bass.

Raider-Roth, M. B. (2005). Trusting what you know: Negotiating the relational context of classroom life. *Teachers College Record, 107*(4), 587–628.

Ramdass, D., & Zimmerman, B. J. (2008). Effects of self-correction strategy training on middle school students' self-efficacy, self-evaluation, and mathematics division learning. *Journal of Advanced Academics, 20*(1), 18–41.

Sadler, R. (1989). Formative assessment and the design of instructional systems. *Instructional Science, 18(2),* 119–144.

Schunk, D. H. (1996). Goal and self-evaluative influences during children's cognitive skill learning. *American Educational Research Journal, 33*(2), 359–382. doi:10.2307/1163289

Tan, K. H. (2008). Qualitatively different ways of experiencing student self-assessment. *Higher Education Research & Development, 27*(1), 15–29.

Zimmerman, B. J. (2002). Becoming a self-regulated learner: An overview. *Theory into Practice, 41*(2), 64–70. doi:10.1207/s15430421tip4102_2

Zimmerman, B. J. (2008). Investigating self-regulation and motivation: Historical background, methodological developments, and future prospects. *American Educational Research Journal, 45*(1), 166–183. doi:10.3102/0002831207312909

2

Self-Assessment, Self-Regulated Learning, and Formative Assessment

The field of self-assessment has grown from two distinct but overlapping areas of research: self-regulated learning (SRL) and formative assessment (Andrade & Brookhart, 2016; Panadero & Alonso-Tapia, 2013). Despite many similarities, these fields have differing foci. Panadero and Alonso-Tapia (2013) explain that although within theories of self-regulation "self-assessment is understood as a process that pupils carry out to self-regulate their learning" (p. 554), within formative assessment, "self-assessment is understood as an instructional process used by the teacher as an educational resource" (p. 554). They note that due to these differing emphases, educators and scholars who view self-assessment from SRL perspectives focus primarily on processes internal to the student, with less emphasis on how self-assessment can and should be used as an instructional strategy within the classroom. Likewise, they argue that those focused on self-assessment as a formative pedagogical strategy often do not devote enough attention to the internal processes within the student. Hence, for the most effective implementation of self-assessment, teachers need to understand and be able to draw on both theoretical approaches.

This chapter explains how self-assessment fits within models of SRL and formative assessment. It describes synergies that integrate the main theoretical rationales behind self-assessment in ways that can help inform practice.

Situating Self-Assessment Within Self-Regulated Learning Theories

SRL theory "is a core conceptual framework to understand the cognitive, motivational, and emotional aspects of learning" (Panadero, 2017, p. 1). It began to develop as a field within educational psychology in the 1980s and continues to be a popular area of research. SRL models place the student self at the center of learning. However, as Boekaerts and Corno (2005) note, "there is no simple and straightforward definition of the construct of self-regulated learning" (p. 199).

SRL is generally considered to have three domains: cognitive, motivational, and affective. There are varying models of self-regulation (e.g., nested, information processing, cyclical), but a cyclical model will be the main focus here because it is well aligned with the formative assessment model discussed in the next section (Andrade & Brookhart, 2016). Zimmerman (2008) defines self-regulated learning as

> the self-directive processes and self-beliefs that enable learners to transform their mental abilities, such as verbal aptitude, into an academic performance skill, such as writing. SRL is viewed as *proactive* processes that students use to acquire academic skill, such as setting goals, selecting and deploying strategies, and self-monitoring one's effectiveness.
>
> (p. 166)

This definition highlights the integration of processes and beliefs within an iterative SRL cycle (i.e., goal setting, followed by strategic actions that are monitored for effectiveness and then evaluated in order to inform goals for the next cycle).

Among those who view SRL as a cyclical process, models differ in how they name and divide the parts of this cycle. Extensively cited work by Zimmerman and colleagues (e.g., Zimmerman, 2008; Zimmerman & Campillo, 2003) divides self-regulated learning into three phases: *forethought*, *performance*, and *self-reflection*. As we explain these, we will also introduce some simpler terminology to describe the phases; it may be useful to share these with your students to help them understand and be able to discuss their own self-regulation of learning. During the forethought phase, learners are *appraising* the task and *planning* goals and actions. During the performance phase, they are *doing* the task and *monitoring* their progress. In the final self-reflection phase, learners are *evaluating* their product and *reflecting* on the reasons for its strengths and weaknesses. Alternative and more technical terms for these phases, which highlight the directionality of the process, are *prospective planning* (forethought), *process* (performance), and *retrospective self-reflection* (self-reflection) (Baars, Vink, van Gog, de Bruin, & Paas, 2014; Dunlosky & Rawson, 2012).

Figure 2.1 illustrates Zimmerman's (2008) cyclical process of SRL, using this simpler terminology. Although many SRL diagrams depict the cycle as a circle, we have chosen instead to place the next cycle above the first cycle in the belief that learners continue to grow and develop their knowledge and skills rather than returning to the same starting point again. This structure acknowledges that although the SRL processes are cyclical, it is hoped that the learning is cumulative and progressive.

One reason why self-assessment is a vital part of self-regulation is that, according to SRL theory, learners have to be able to continuously identify problems and adjust their use of strategies and level

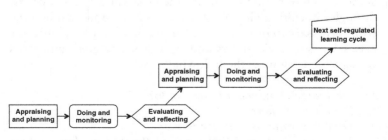

Figure 2.1 A Cyclical Model of Self-Regulated Learning
Source: Based on Zimmerman, 2008.

of effort when circumstances and/or goals change. When these adjustments help the learner get closer to chosen goals, they are considered *adaptive*. For example, a learner might decide to put in more effort when a task becomes challenging or try a new and potentially more effective strategy. However, changes that interfere with goal attainment are called *maladaptive*. For example, a learner might choose to persist with a strategy that is clearly not working or decide to stop trying because the task is "too hard."

Self-regulating students monitor the effectiveness of their approaches to learning, making changes as necessary, maximizing the possibility of adaptive courses of action. Hence, "self-assessment influences all stages of the self-regulatory process" (Panadero & Alonso-Tapia, 2013, p. 557). As Brookhart (2016) explained, "Self-assessment is in the warp and woof of self-regulated learning. Self-assessment has the same boundaries of meaning as the phases of self-regulated learning (i.e., goals, monitoring, adjusting, and reflecting)" (p. 362). Thus, self-assessment is a key component of how students become aware of and subsequently regulate their thoughts, feelings, and behaviors in order to fulfill their ambitions throughout all parts of a learning cycle.

For example, when *appraising* and *planning* (forethought), the learner analyzes the task, which leads to goal setting and strategic planning. Whether students are consciously aware of it or not, they assess the value of the task, evaluate their own goals, and plan how much time and effort they will commit. Self-motivation beliefs are activated (e.g., self-efficacy, outcome expectations, task interest/value, control perceptions, goal orientation). The importance of motivation cannot be underestimated. Students' interest in and value for the task will help them persist through difficulties, allowing them to exercise and maintain the effort necessary to be successful. During this first phase, students may self-assess their understanding of learning goals and tasks with such questions as the following:

- *Do I understand what I have to do?*
- *Do I have a plan?*
- *How important is this task to me?*
- *How confident am I that I can do this task within the time and parameters specified?*

When *doing* and *monitoring* (performance phase), learners work to complete the actual task or learning while simultaneously monitoring and self-assessing their progress, particularly around the effectiveness and efficiency of their learning strategies. This requires them to exercise self-control, focus their attention, and employ task strategies, drawing on self-instruction (i.e., instructions they give to themselves about how to complete the task) and imagery (i.e., mental organization of information). As they are doing the task, students examine their work to determine if current practices are likely to allow them to reach their personal goals and/or to meet external expectations and standards. They may compare their performance to examples, expert models, rubrics, or standards and use metacognitive monitoring and self-recording skills (e.g., keeping track of actions for later examination). Students may use self-assessment to provide themselves with formative feedback on their progress by asking such questions as the following:

- *How am I progressing toward my learning goal?*
- *Are the strategies I am using working?*
- *Is my work at the level of quality I am hoping to achieve?*
- *What can I do to improve my work?*
- *Do I need to seek help from a peer or the teacher?*

After the task is finished, students engage in *evaluating* their work and *reflecting* on reasons for strengths and weaknesses (self-reflection phase). This evaluation is likely to spark a range of achievement emotions (e.g., pride, relief, disappointment) (Vogl & Pekrun, 2016). In this phase, students are likely to attribute particular reasons for their own success or failure. For example, here are some of the ways New Zealand teacher Imogen's year 8 students justified their own successes and failures via written self-assessment comments:

- *"I didn't complete it because I thought to* [sic] *long about what I was going to say."*
- *"I think I have done a really good job today because I made myself organized in my book and I did a lot of work."*
- *"I was successful because I was focused."*

These reflections can foster the development of an adaptive growth orientation (e.g., *I think I could do this even better if I put in more effort*) or a maladaptive ego-protective orientation (e.g., *I didn't do well, but that's okay because this subject isn't important*). During this phase, student self-assessments may focus on summative evaluation of their efforts (e.g., *How good is the result I achieved?*) but may also develop feedback that can be used formatively within their next task (e.g., *What do I need to work on next? What should I do differently next time?*). Although some models of SRL tend to locate self-assessment primarily within this final phase, it is our view, along with many other authors, such as Andrade and Valtcheva (2009) and Boekaerts and Corno (2005), that self-assessment should occur within all phases of the learning cycle.

Self-assessment is particularly important for SRL because it provides learners with feedback that enables them to reach learning goals. Butler and Winne (1995) argue that "for all self-regulated activities, feedback is an inherent catalyst" (p. 246). Students often draw on feedback from external sources (e.g., teacher, peer, computer, worked example, previous test score) when formulating their self-assessments about their progress (Yan & Brown, 2017). As Dinsmore and Wilson (2016) note, "Self-assessment with contextually situated evaluator feedback has the largest potential to increase the likelihood of self-regulatory activity on the part of the learner, thereby improving learning and performance" (p. 149).

Although external feedback can provide students with alternative points of view and potentially access to higher levels of expertise, particularly when received from teachers and peers, self-assessment feedback may be especially valuable for several reasons. First, as students provides it to themselves, it can be delivered just in time wherever and whenever it is needed. This is in contrast to the inevitable delay in seeking feedback from an external source. The speed of feedback in self-testing (i.e., taking an objectively scored test for and by oneself) is a major reason that it is so widely accepted as a useful study technique (Robinson, 1970) and why so many consider it as the quintessential form of self-assessment (Deneen, 2014).

Second, numerous studies have identified that students may find external feedback difficult to understand (for multiple reasons, including indecipherable teacher handwriting, ambiguous phrasing, use of jargon, lack of specificity, etc.) (Hattie & Timperley, 2007). Additionally, students may misinterpret feedback (i.e., miss the main messages the feedback sender intended) or may not find responses within the feedback to the questions personally important to them (Hattie & Timperley, 2007). In contrast, student self-created feedback will use understandable language and will be focused on the self's own specific questions or issues. Finally, although it may be relatively easy for students to judge external feedback as irrelevant or inaccurate, it is much harder for them to disregard or ignore their own feedback.

Building on Figure 2.1, Figure 2.2 provides added detail about how the cyclical model works, showing that throughout SRL processes, self-assessment plays a key role. Within this model, learners self-assess the learning or task demands and criteria before establishing goals and creating a plan for their learning. Within K–12 schooling, self-regulation is usually in response to tasks set by the curriculum and the teacher, but this process could equally apply to any learning the student undertakes independently. While learning, self-assessment becomes a form

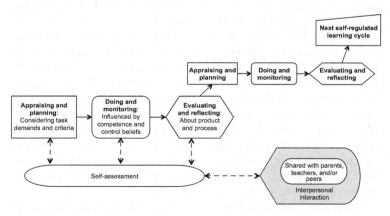

Figure 2.2 The Goal and Process of Self-Assessment

of metacognitive monitoring of the processes used to achieve the learning goal. That monitoring is influenced by the learner's various competence and control beliefs (e.g., motivations, goals, attributions, self-efficacy). In classroom contexts, self-assessment is usually shared with the teacher and sometimes with classmates, as shown by the dashed lines, but this is not always the case. Their reactions and comments then interact with the learner's own internal sensations, perceptions, and thoughts to confirm or revise the original self-assessment. Once the learning is finished, the student is expected to retrospectively assess both the learning product and the learning processes to inform subsequent improvements in capabilities and outcomes.

Although the cognitive component of SRL is vital, affect and motivation play a critical role. Panadero and Alonso-Tapia (2013) suggest that Zimmerman's (2008) SRL model does not sufficiently address student emotion. Boekaerts and colleagues' (Boekaerts, 1997; Boekaerts & Corno, 2005) dual-processing model examines more explicitly how student affective responses and mind-sets may influence their self-regulatory decisions, making it useful to explore. This model of self-regulation highlights that students generally have two main objectives: growth in learning and/or protection or enhancement of their egos. These goals are often in conflict because growth requires the learner to identify and accept weakness or failure in work as a basis for improvement. This means that the student has to (a) be resilient enough to acknowledge and accept mistakes, (b) make sure emotional responses to "failure" do not lead to decreased motivation for improvement, and (c) accept the responsibility of regulating future action to overcome those weaknesses. When students focus on their emotional well-being (i.e., avoid the negative emotions associated with acknowledging mistakes) or deny responsibility (i.e., externalize failure as not being their fault), they engage in practices, thoughts, and motivations that maximize ego protection or enhancement. Engagement in self-regulated learning requires a commitment to a growth-oriented pathway rather than to the protection of the ego.

Clearly, students need to be more focused on academic growth than ego protection if they are to succeed in meeting learning goals set by schools, teachers, parents, and the curriculum. However, the importance of student emotional and psychological welfare cannot be ignored in this process. Classroom practices must help students to develop and maintain personal well-being (e.g., promote pride in self, facilitate positive social standing within the classroom, protect from inappropriate or unnecessary threats to identity or ego, and assist in the acquisition of skills and resources).

It is important to understand that an overemphasis on well-being goals may undermine growth-oriented learning goals. For example, a student may want to improve knowledge (growth goal) but be hesitant to exert effort for fear of replicating previous experiences of failure. Such a stance would lead students to protect their self-esteem (i.e., a well-being goal) at the expense of learning. Students may avoid asking a peer for help (sometimes necessary to achieve growth goals) because of concern that others will think less of them. Within the context of self-assessment, an overemphasis on well-being goals has the potential to undermine self-assessment validity and realism because students may not want to acknowledge problems within their work to the teacher, peers, or themselves. Additionally, well-being goals may encourage some students to avoid self-assessment altogether for fear of discovering and having to admit to failure (e.g., *What if I find out my work is of really poor quality?*) or because they are concerned that disclosing their weaknesses may cause their teacher or peers to ridicule or think less of them.

It is vital to understand that student well-being goals can significantly undermine student engagement in self-assessment and its realism (Andrade & Brown, 2016; Brown, Andrade, & Chen, 2015). This problem is not unique to children as learners. For example, teachers are sometimes reluctant to seek help when struggling with a difficult class or to admit that their own teaching may be adding to the learners' difficulties. Such admission, particularly in a high-accountability environment, may result in negative consequences (e.g., diminished standing, employment implications), even though the most constructive response would be offers of assistance and professional development. A reluctance to engage in a growth pathway is a normal part of the human condition. Hence, an obvious precondition for effective self-assessment is a social environment that prizes growth while minimizing unnecessary threats to the ego, something discussed further in Chapters 3 and 5.

In summary, self-assessment is explicitly mentioned in SRL theory (albeit often by other names, such as self-monitoring), and self-assessment can support all stages of the self-regulation cycle. However, there is still work to be done to make self-assessment's role within the self-regulation of learning more explicit. Dinsmore and Wilson (2016) noted that self-regulation throughout and after assessment is contingent on a variety of factors, including the learner's developmental characteristics, the nature of the task and domain, and the type of outcome desired (i.e., cognitive, motivational, and/or behavioral). Hence, although self-assessment is certainly named within the SRL literature and is an encouraged practice, these mitigating factors remain largely underexplored.

Situating Self-Assessment Within Formative Assessment

The current international focus on formative assessment, especially within compulsory schooling sectors, has been strongly influenced by the United Kingdom's Assessment Reform Group (Assessment Reform Group, 1999; Black & Wiliam, 1998a, 1998b; Black, Harrison, Lee, Marshall, & Wiliam, 2003, Leahy, Lyon, Thompson, & Wiliam, 2005). This group has actively promoted self-assessment as a potentially valuable formative strategy within the global assessment for learning movement. In fact, Black et al. (2003) argue, "It is very difficult for students to achieve a learning goal unless they understand that goal and can assess what they need to do to reach it. So self-assessment is essential to learning" (p. 49).

Although there is general agreement that formative assessment is beneficial, how it is defined varies widely, and these variations have implications for self-assessment's design and use as a formative practice. Although some common elements connect most definitions of formative assessment, as Bennett (2011) explained, "the term, 'formative assessment', does not yet represent a well-defined set of artefacts or practices" (p. 5). The term *formative assessment* initially appeared in Scriven's (1967) work in program evaluation. His definition focused on assessment's timing—formative assessment took place early enough to make a difference to the process or product, while summative took place at the end of the process. Other authors (e.g., Sadler, 1989) argued that it was the purpose and effects of the assessment that determined if it was or was not formative (rather than timing). Such scholars seem to suggest that particular types of assessment commonly used for accountability or certification processes (e.g., standardized tests) are unlikely to be formative.

Some have an even more restrictive definition of formative assessment. For example, Swaffield (2011) has gone so far as to suggest that only the in-the-moment, on-the-fly student interactions with one another and the teacher should be considered formative, while Carless (2015) has recently proposed that the term should refer only to assessment practices where there is clear evidence of positive direct effects on students' learning. Clearly, some of these definitions exclude practices often considered to be examples of self-assessment (e.g., according to Swaffield's, 2011 definition, more formal self-marking exercises would not be considered formative).

Despite these differences, formative assessment definitions agree that such assessments should be used to improve learning outcomes during the process of learning rather than as a method for evaluating students, teachers, or schools. A major principle of assessment for learning (Black et al., 2003; Stiggins, 2005) is that students should actively engage with curricular targets and monitor their progress toward these goals, as these processes will help them learn more. To do this, some form of assessment needs to occur during the process of learning, generating feedback that arrives before any grades or marks and that directs the learner's efforts to improved performance within the task. Although student involvement in and use of assessment is a vital component of formative practice, there is also a legitimate space, in our opinion, for formative assessment to inform the teacher. If designed to answer the question "Who needs to be taught what next?" (Brown & Hattie, 2012), formative assessment results can help teachers to better tailor instruction and learning experiences to maximize student progress.

Additionally, like self-assessment, formative assessment processes do have student self-regulation as a major goal. When students receive formative feedback from themselves, peers, and/or the teacher during the learning process, they have the opportunity to self-regulate their learning. It is expected that this feedback will help the student during the process of learning, leading to better task completion (Nicol & Macfarlane-Dick, 2006). This is in contrast to feedback (e.g., comments or grades) given after a task is completed (i.e., summative or assessment *of* learning). Although summative feedback may have some value for future learning, it is considered too late to support changes that might increase the quality of the student's work in that instance. For example, in one of our studies, Joe, a New Zealand high school student, explained it this way: "*You want the comments, but if it's the last step and you're not going to get another chance at it, then you may as well just have a grade.*"

One challenge for those working in the area of formative assessment is that unlike the field of self-regulated learning (which has always been heavily grounded in educational psychology theory), work on formative assessment has followed a different path. Black and Wiliam (2009) note that their initial work on the topic (i.e., Black & Wiliam, 1998a, 1998b) was not based on any specific theoretical perspective; instead, they sought to pragmatically identify classroom practices they considered to be formative and to explore the impact these might have on student learning. Stobart (2006) has suggested that assessment for learning was specifically a function of the English-speaking world's primary schooling approach to child-centered education. Although later work (e.g., Black & Wiliam, 2009; Wiliam, 2010) has attempted to create a more cohesive theoretical foundation for formative assessment, because there are diverse practices that teachers and academics label as formative, it is reasonable to expect quite different results from various techniques. This is particularly the case when formative practices are deployed in differing contexts and in quite different ways. Hence, having a stronger theoretical foundation would potentially help educators understand and explain varying effects.

Despite variation in definitions and theoretical underpinnings around the concept of formative assessment, formative uses of self-assessment, where students use self-assessment to provide themselves with feedback before having to undergo any formal evaluation of their work, are promoted as being of most value (Andrade, 2010). Receiving this feedback during a task (and learning cycle) is thought to be particularly powerful because it allows learners the opportunity to gain insights early enough to lead to improvement as they continue working on the task. Figure 2.3 shows how self-assessment fits into a learning cycle according to formative assessment models. In these, self-assessment activities are usually anchored to a particular task. The observable task setting, performance, completion, and evaluation are shown with solid lines. In contrast, the less visible self-assessments, peer and teacher feedback, and interaction between the self and others are portrayed with dashed lines relative to the task process.

Self-assessment in this context involves relating current work to task criteria and standards, perhaps aided by supporting materials, such as exemplars or rubrics, or drawing on feedback from previous efforts. Here the self-assessment takes place during the learning, and students have a chance to use the feedback to improve before the work is formally evaluated or graded. As Andrade and Brookhart (2016) note, the sequential processes advocated for within classroom assessment (i.e., goal setting, monitoring via feedback, and revision or adjustment; Figure 2.3)

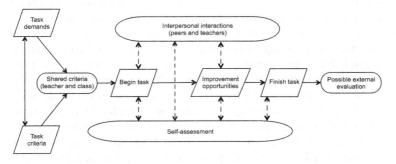

Figure 2.3 Self-Assessment Within Formative Assessment

align well with the phases of a cycle of self-regulated learning (i.e., forethought, performance, and self-reflection; Zimmerman, 2008).

However, studies of actual classroom self-assessment practice have identified that relationships between the learner and his or her teacher and peers can pose serious challenges to the validity of self-assessment (Cowie, 2005; Harris & Brown, 2013). Students have reported sharing purposefully inaccurate self-assessments (e.g., over- or undervaluing their work, making comments the student knows are false) when they believe the classroom environment is not psychologically safe (this issue is discussed further in Chapter 3).

Like SRL theory, formative assessment positions the student as a key agent in the learning process. However, the assessment for learning movement has generally not developed well-designed sequences and recommendations for self-assessment implementation, perhaps because it promotes such a plethora of practices, each of which can be implemented in a multitude of ways.

To illustrate the vastly different approaches to formative assessment, consider the distinction Pryor and Crossouard (2008) draw between convergent and divergent forms of formative assessment. In convergent approaches, "formative assessment was a means by which teachers orchestrated the construction of a lesson text, marking out a correct train of thought for the students to appropriate" (p. 4). Here students receive teacher feedback during their learning, but interactions are focused on quizzing students to ensure they acquire curricular knowledge and guiding them to a correct answer. Clearly, such environments allow fairly limited opportunities for meaningful self-assessment.

In contrast, in divergent formative assessment practices, teachers ask probing and open-ended questions and co-construct knowledge with students rather than constraining student participation to the authorized knowledge of the curriculum. In these environments, formative assessment would include self- and/or peer assessment as ways of generating feedback and new ideas rather than functioning as a grading or evaluative process.

Even if a divergent approach to formative assessment is adopted, teachers may or may not choose to include self-assessment tasks in their classrooms. A further challenge for effective formative self-assessment use is that it is often presented as a smorgasbord of roughly equivalent practices with equal merit and applicability (e.g., Traffic Lights, self-testing, rating against a rubric). Some caution about this grab-bag approach has been advised (Andrade & Brown, 2016), and we have advocated that a curriculum around self-assessment is needed to help teachers select developmentally appropriate practices and to assist students to build the competence and complexity of their self-assessment abilities over time (Brown & Harris, 2014).

In summary, it is important to understand that not all enacted practices teachers describe as formative align well with or privilege self-assessment. Other formative techniques include peer assessment, comment-only marking, interactive teacher questioning, and setting learning intentions and success criteria, to name just a few. Hence, it is very possible to enact formative assessment practices without drawing on self-assessment at all.

Integrating Self-Assessment With Self-Regulated Learning and Formative Assessment

Although formative assessment and self-regulated learning theories have different origins, they both position the student as a key agent within learning and assessment situations. Additionally, as Andrade and Brookhart (2016) note, "clear learning goals and criteria are the foundation on which both formative assessment and SRL rest" (p. 304).

It is useful to consider how these two frameworks might be integrated around self-assessment. Figure 2.4 represents our understanding of how the key processes from SRL and formative assessment apply to self-assessment in a teacher-led classroom context and in relation to a specific task. Again, the solid lines portray the task process initiated by the teacher, leading to an end-of-work evaluation of some sort. The dashed lines show the complex relationships between the task and the internal self-regulatory and self-assessment activities of the learner. We have bracketed the process of shared criteria about a task, its performance, and any possible interpersonal feedback and

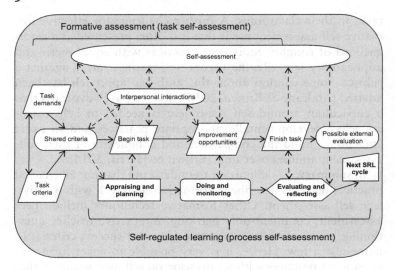

Figure 2.4 Self-Assessment Embedded in Formative Assessment and Self-Regulated Learning

self-assessment under formative assessment, as these are commonly advocated for within assessment for learning (Leahy et al., 2005). Note that the formative assessment bracket includes self-assessment but not possible external evaluation, even though self-assessment can be used to generate summative evaluation.

The self-regulated learning bracket at the bottom of the diagram illustrates that once a task is set, the self-regulating student engages actively in the process of planning, metacognitively monitoring, evaluating, and reflecting on task outcomes and processes. Once students are presented with task demands and expectations, students begin by appraising the task: *What is it that I have to do? Is this task important to me?* As part of this process, according to formative assessment principles, students and the teacher may collaboratively generate or deconstruct criteria and standards describing a successful performance. This discussion triggers students' planning for the task and the self-assessment of their personal goals, motivations, competence, and control over internal factors in relation to the task.

Next, students start actually doing the task. As work on the task proceeds, students can assess the quality of the work relative to criteria and standards, monitoring the strategies and behaviors being used to achieve the task. Students engage in metacognitive monitoring, including self-assessment, which helps them to check their own progress and, hopefully, maintain motivation to continue the learning and task. Thorough self-assessment helps students identify where further work is needed, allowing them to choose and apply appropriate strategies to help them improve. This formative feedback gives learners extra opportunities to identify and respond to weaknesses before they are subjected to any external evaluation. Formative feedback from external sources (e.g., peers, teacher, answer sheets, model responses, computers) can help learners evaluate the alignment of their own self-assessments with external feedback and may also lead to productive revisions in the work. This feedback may be about the work itself, but it could also be about the learner's self-assessment (e.g., *I agree/disagree with your self-assessment because . . .*).

After the work is completed, learners can then use self-assessment to retrospectively reflect on the quality of their work and to identify if task goals have been reached. Although this kind of terminal self-assessment cannot lead to progress on the actual task because it has already been completed, it could feed into planning for the next task. Summative self-assessment in this self-reflection phase can be useful for helping students understand their current levels of proficiency, allowing them to identify particular aspects of their work that require improvement and, hopefully, the strategies they might adopt in the future to move forward.

Although in Figure 2.4 the focus is on the learner and his or her use of self-assessment in relation to a particular task, it is vital to remember that self-assessment within compulsory, as well as higher, education takes place in a complex social environment. The shaded background of the diagram highlights the social and psychological space in which student self-assessment takes place. These intra- and inter-psychological processes may include such features as internal maladaptive competence and control beliefs, inappropriate ego protection, and personality and cultural factors that result in unrealistic self-assessments. Given the importance of peer interaction in formative assessment, unhealthy relationships within the classroom can lead to distorted self-assessments. Students' concerns about their social standing within the classroom (e.g., not wanting to appear too successful or less competent than others) may prompt them to manipulate their own self-assessments to conform to their perceptions of peer expectations. Likewise, students' perceptions of teacher or parent expectations and probable reactions may also encourage them to provide unrealistic or purposefully inaccurate evaluations of their work. Note also that Figure 2.4 is a greatly simplified portrayal of complex self-assessment interactions between the student and the task, drawing on models of formative assessment and self-regulated learning. We welcome feedback on how this figure could be improved.

Summary

This chapter introduced the historical backgrounds and theoretical frameworks commonly used to underpin self-assessment approaches within the classroom. In the first section, we focused on Zimmerman's (2008) cyclical model of self-regulated learning where students engage in forethought, performance, and self-reflective phases within cycles of learning. This model reminds us of the importance of drawing on self-assessment in all phases of learning in order to maximize self-regulation. In the first phase where students are planning their approach to the learning or task, they should be encouraged to self-assess in ways that help them identify their goals, motivation, and current strengths and weaknesses in relation to the task, allowing them to select appropriate strategies and areas of focus. As they are completing the task, students should continue to monitor their progress against expectations, allowing them to identify problems and troubleshoot as they go. Finally, once the task or cycle of learning is complete, it is important for students to draw on self-assessment to reflect on the final product and to identify their next learning steps, as these will feed into the forethought phase of their next cycle of learning.

This section of the chapter also introduced you to Boekaerts and her colleagues' dual-processing model of self-regulation, which acknowledges that students may aim to achieve both growth and well-being goals. Particularly within the context of self-assessment, student concerns about ego protection (that is, for most, a strong well-being goal) may undermine their willingness to honestly self-assess their progress or may encourage them to respond in dishonest ways due to fear of parent, teacher, or peer reactions to their honest opinions about their work. Hence, students have to be actively encouraged to value growth over ego protection, and classrooms must be safe places where students can acknowledge shortcomings within the current iteration of their work.

The second section related self-assessment to formative assessment, particularly as promoted via the global assessment for learning movement. It highlighted that formative assessment encourages student agency within the learning process but that within this approach, self-assessment is just one of the many techniques teachers could draw on to generate formative feedback for their learners. Like a cycle of self-regulated learning, formative assessment is part of a cyclical process, but key authors acknowledge that this movement has been empirically rather than theoretically driven, with theoretical framing being a more recent addition to the field.

The final section provided a model of self-assessment that we believe brings together the key ideas from both the formative assessment and the self-assessment literatures. This model shows the three main phases of learning where self-assessment should be applied:

1. *Appraising and planning.* Students initially unpack the task, form opinions about its purpose and value, set personal goals, and plan for the task or cycle of learning.
2. *Doing and monitoring.* Students work on the task and monitor progress. This monitoring helps students to identify what is and is not going well, allowing them to decide if current

strategies are working and to make necessary adjustments to effort and approach.

3. *Evaluating and reflecting.* Students evaluate their final product or understanding against expectations to determine how well they met goals, identifying areas to work on next time.

This model highlights the psychosocial backdrop to classroom self-assessment practices and identifies the role of external feedback from teachers, parents, peers, computer sources, and documents within the self-assessment process. This psychosocial space and its implications for self-assessment will be further discussed in Chapter 3.

References

Andrade, H. (2010). Students as the definitive source of formative assessment: Academic self-assessment and the self-regulation of learning. In H. L. Andrade & G. J. Cizek (Eds.), *Handbook of formative assessment* (pp. 90–105). New York, NY: Routledge.

Andrade, H., & Brookhart, S. M. (2016). The role of classroom assessment in supporting self-regulated learning. In D. Laveault & L. Allal (Eds.), *Assessment for learning: Meeting the challenge of implementation* (pp. 293–309). Cham, Switzerland: Springer International.

Andrade, H., & Brown, G. T. L. (2016). Student self-assessment in the classroom. In G. T. L. Brown & L. R. Harris (Eds.), *Handbook of human and social conditions in assessment* (pp. 319–334). New York, NY: Routledge.

Andrade, H., & Valtcheva, A. (2009). Promoting learning and achievement through self-assessment. *Theory into Practice, 28*(1), 12–19.

Assessment Reform Group. (1999). *Assessment for learning: Beyond the black box.* Retrieved from www.nuffieldfoundation.org/sites/default/files/files/beyond_blackbox.pdf

Baars, M., Vink, S., van Gog, T., de Bruin, A., & Paas, F. (2014). Effects of training self-assessment and using assessment standards on retrospective and prospective monitoring of problem solving. *Learning & Instruction, 33,* 92–107. doi:10.1016/j.learninstruc.2014.04.004

Bennett, R. E. (2011). Formative assessment: A critical review. *Assessment in Education: Principles, Policy & Practice, 18*(1), 5–25. doi:10.1080/0969594x.2010.513678

Black, P., Harrison, C., Lee, C., Marshall, B., & Wiliam, D. (2003). *Assessment for learning: Putting it into practice*. Maidenhead, England: Open University Press.

Black, P., & Wiliam, D. (1998a). Assessment and classroom learning. *Assessment in Education, 5*(1), 7–74.

Black, P., & Wiliam, D. (1998b). *Inside the black box: Raising standards through classroom assessment*. London, England: Department of Education and Professional Studies, King's College London.

Black, P., & Wiliam, D. (2009). Developing the theory of formative assessment. *Educational Assessment, Evaluation and Accountability, 21*(1), 5–31.

Boekaerts, M. (1997). Self-regulated learning: A new concept embraced by researchers, policy makers, educators, teachers, and students. *Learning and Instruction, 7*, 161–186. doi: https://doi.org/10.1016/S0959-4752(96)00015-1

Boekaerts, M., & Corno, L. (2005). Self-regulation in the classroom: A perspective on assessment and intervention. *Applied Psychology, 54*(2), 199–231. doi:10.1111/j.1464-0597.2005.00205

Brookhart, S. M. (2016). Building assessments that work in the classroom. In G. T. L. Brown & L. R. Harris (Eds.), *Handbook of human and social conditions in assessment* (pp. 351–365). New York, NY: Routledge.

Brown, G. T. L., Andrade, H., & Chen, F. (2015). Accuracy in student self-assessment: Directions and cautions for research. *Assessment in Education: Principles, Policy & Practice, 22*(4), 444–457. doi:10.1080/0969594X.2014.996523

Brown, G. T. L., & Harris, L. R. (2014). The future of self-assessment in classroom practice: Reframing self-assessment as a core competency. *Frontline Learning Research, 3*, 22–30. doi:10.14786/flr.v2i1.24

Brown, G. T. L., & Hattie, J. A. (2012). The benefits of regular standardized assessment in childhood education: Guiding improved instruction and learning. In S. Suggate & E. Reese (Eds.), *Contemporary debates in childhood education and development* (pp. 287–292). London, England: Routledge.

Butler, D. L., & Winne, P. H. (1995). Feedback and self-regulated learning: A theoretical synthesis. *Review of Educational Research, 65*(3), 245–281.

Carless, D. (2015). Exploring learning-oriented assessment processes. *Higher Education, 69*(6), 963–976. doi:10.1007/s10734-014-9816-z

Cowie, B. (2005). Pupil commentary on assessment for learning. *Curriculum Journal, 16*(2), 137–151.

Deneen, C. C. (2014). How good am I? Self-evaluation in an examination culture. In J. Curry & P. Hanstedt (Eds.), *Reading Hong Kong, reading ourselves* (pp. 230–249). Hong Kong, China: City University of Hong Kong Press.

Dinsmore, D. L., & Wilson, H. E. (2016). Student participation in assessment: Does it influence self-regulation? In G. T. L. Brown & L. R. Harris (Eds.), *Handbook of human and social conditions in assessment* (pp. 145–168). New York, NY: Routledge.

Dunlosky, J., & Rawson, K. A. (2012). Overconfidence produces underachievement: Inaccurate self-evaluations undermine students' learning and retention. *Learning & Instruction*, 22(4), 271–280. doi:10.1016/j.learninstruc.2011.08.003

Harris, L. R., & Brown, G. T. L. (2013). Opportunities and obstacles to consider when using peer- and self-assessment to improve student learning: Case studies into teachers' implementation. *Teaching and Teacher Education*, 36, 101–111. doi:10.1016/j.tate.2013.07.008

Hattie, J., & Timperley, H. (2007). The power of feedback. *Review of Educational Research*, 77(1), 81–112.

Leahy, S., Lyon, C., Thompson, M., & Wiliam, D. (2005). Classroom assessment: Minute by minute, day by day. *Educational Leadership*, 63(3), 19–24.

Nicol, D. J., & Macfarlane-Dick, D. (2006). Formative assessment and self-regulated learning: A model and seven principles of good feedback practice. *Studies in Higher Education*, 31(2), 199–218.

Panadero, E. (2017). A review of self-regulated learning: Six models and four directions for research. *Frontiers in Psychology*, 8, 1–28. doi:10.3389/fpsyg.2017.00422

Panadero, E., & Alonso-Tapia, J. (2013). Self-assessment: Theoretical and practical connotations: When it happens, how is it acquired and what to do to develop it in our students. *Electronic Journal of Research in Educational Psychology*, 11(2), 551–576.

Pryor, J., & Crossouard, B. (2008). A socio-cultural theorisation of formative assessment. *Oxford Review of Education*, 34(1), 1–20. doi:10.1080/03054980701476386

Robinson, F. P. (1970). *Effective study* (4th ed.). New York, NY: Harper & Row.

Sadler, R. (1989). Formative assessment and the design of instructional systems. *Instructional Science*, 18, 119–144.

Scriven, M. (1967). The methodology of evaluation. In R. Tyler, R. Gagne, & M. Scriven (Eds.), *Perspectives on curriculum evaluation* (pp. 39–84). Chicago, IL: Rand McNally.

Stiggins, R. J. (2005). *Student-involved assessment for learning* (4th ed.). Upper Saddle River, NJ: Pearson Education.

Stobart, G. (2006). The validity of formative assessment. In J. Gardner (Ed.), *Assessment and learning* (pp. 133–146). London, England: Sage.

Swaffield, S. (2011). Getting to the heart of authentic assessment for learning. *Assessment in Education: Principles, Policy & Practice*, *18*(4), 433–449.

Vogl, E., & Pekrun, R. (2016). Emotions that matter to achievement: Student feelings about assessment. In G. T. L. Brown & L. R. Harris (Eds.), *Handbook of human and social conditions in assessment* (pp. 111–128). New York, NY: Routledge.

Wiliam, D. (2010). An integrative summary of the research literature and implications for a new theory of formative assessment. In H. Andrade & G. J. Cizek (Eds.), *Handbook of formative assessment* (pp. 18–40). New York, NY: Routledge.

Yan, Z., & Brown, G. T. L. (2017). A cyclical self-assessment process: Towards a model of how students engage in self-assessment. *Assessment & Evaluation in Higher Education*, *42*(8), 1247–1262. doi:10.1080/02602938.2016.1260091

Zimmerman, B. J. (2008). Investigating self-regulation and motivation: Historical background, methodological developments, and future prospects. *American Educational Research Journal*, *45*(1), 166–183. doi:10.3102/0002831207312909

Zimmerman, B. J., & Campillo, M. (2003). Motivating self-regulated problem solvers. In J. E. Davidson & R. J. Sternberg (Eds.), *The nature of problem solving* (pp. 233–262). New York, NY: Cambridge University Press.

3

Challenges When Implementing Self-Assessment

Although there is evidence that self-assessment can improve student learning (Brown & Harris, 2013), it can be difficult to implement self-assessment in ways that make this promise a reality. This chapter discusses common difficulties teachers may encounter when implementing self-assessment in the classroom, along with strategies and tips to mitigate these problems. Each of the following challenges will be addressed:

- Getting students to take responsibility for self-assessment processes
- Making complex learning objectives transparent
- Creating a psychologically safe environment for self-assessment
- Moving beyond the ego and minimizing negative student conceptions
- Improving the accuracy and validity of student self-assessments
- Getting students to act on self-assessment data

Getting Students to Take Responsibility for Self-Assessment Processes

One major challenge for employing effective self-assessment is dismantling the power hierarchy embedded in assessment more broadly. In this conventional hierarchy, the teacher is the expert and source of knowledge; it is his or her job to set the agenda within the classroom, monitor student progress, and provide evaluation and feedback. Teachers usually initiate assessment processes (e.g., ask questions or set tests), receive student responses, and then evaluate the accuracy and sufficiency of those responses (Torrance & Pryor, 1998). This process is often expressed as Initiate-Respond-Evaluate (I-R-E) (Mehan, 1979). Teacher correction and evaluation may stereotypically occur through the use of the infamous red pen on student assignments and tests.

However, even during interactive, interpersonal assessment, I-R-E sequence processes can take place (e.g., a teacher informally asks a student a question, the student answers, and then the teacher provides evaluation by praising, silencing, or correcting the student's response or responding via gestures and facial expressions). In their extensive review of effective pedagogical practices, Sinnema and Aitken (2012) emphasize the importance of creating a classroom community in which teachers share power with students, a finding that has clear implications for those planning to use self-assessment. Although the teacher should rightly be expected to provide expert knowledge and leadership within the classroom, if students have no say in or control over assessment, several unfortunate, often unintended, consequences are likely.

First, students may feel disempowered in relation to assessment (e.g., Reay & Wiliam, 1999), seeing assessment as something that is done to them rather than with or by them. In most cases, when students complete an assessment, they have no say over its format, timing, or administrative conditions or any input into how the results are reported. As one second grade student put it, the teacher "*gives us a SHEET and we must do the tasks she tells us, and then we have to show her and she SEES what we have learnt*" (Remesal, 2009, p. 40).

Furthermore, students are not in a position to prevent the teacher from seeing their book work or homework within which they may have recorded a self-assessment. For example, consider the anecdote Cowie (2009) shared:

> One student said her teacher would demand to see her book if she tried to withhold it stating, *"You can't really say, 'No, you're not allowed to look at my work.' She'll [the teacher] just say, 'Yes I am.'"*
>
> (p. 95, italics added)

Many studies have identified that students feel disempowered, especially in relation to mandated external assessments and examinations that are used to evaluate them or their schools (e.g., Nichols & Berliner, 2007; Wheelock, Bebell, & Haney, 2000). This sense of disempowerment can even be seen in pictures of assessment drawn by university-level students (Brown & Wang, 2013). Within the classroom, students are seldom offered meaningful opportunities for choice around how they demonstrate their learning; standardization means that everyone usually has to do the same task under the same conditions, except in rare cases when teachers actually practice quality differentiation as described by Tomlinson and Moon (2013).

Second, most students have not been encouraged to view themselves as capable of providing meaningful academic feedback about their work. Within our own research, students have said things like *"I think my teacher's judgment matters more than mine"* and *"It's pretty much the teacher's judgment that really counts"* (Harris & Brown, 2013, p. 109), which are similar to comments recorded by other researchers, such as *"It's better to see what someone else has to say about you than what you think about yourself"* (Peterson & Irving, 2008, p. 245). These comments indicate clearly that some students believe that only the teacher has the knowledge or authority to evaluate student work. As a result, some students resist self-assessment (and peer-assessment) practices because they see evaluation as the sole responsibility of the teacher (Harris & Brown, 2013; Ross, 2006; Sadler & Good, 2006). For example, a student in one of our studies said he had been made to self-assess because "*our teacher ran out of time [to assess our work], so we just did it*" (Harris & Brown, 2013, p. 108), implying that his teacher was shirking her responsibilities by making students self-assess. Parents may also have the view that teachers should hold sole responsibility for assessment (Ross, 2006).

Finally, students may resist the extra work self-assessment requires. For example, one Year 10 boy in Cowie's (2005) study noted, "*I hate it when you ask how to do something and they ask us questions back. They [teachers] should just tell us what to do so we can get on*" (p. 143). These attitudes are particularly prevalent among students who adopt performance approaches to learning (Cowie, 2009). Hence, many students are highly dependent on their teachers for feedback, which is particularly problematic in contexts where there are relatively high student to teacher ratios (e.g., high school contexts, countries such as China) and in tertiary education or workplace learning where students are expected to operate more independently.

External accountability systems can also reinforce this conventional view of assessment. In school contexts where external evaluation scores matter, teachers feel extreme pressure to make sure they cover and evaluate content in the particular ways the system values (Nichols & Berliner, 2007; Nichols & Harris, 2016), leaving little room for student evaluation and choice. Although self-assessment provides opportunities for long-term academic growth, it is time consuming to set up and administer; thus, it competes for classroom time. It is much "easier" for the teacher to give an answer than to require students to work it out for themselves. Likewise, it is faster to test students than to ask them to judge their own work and to read or listen to their justifications for their self-assessments. Thus, teachers may find it safer to provide answers and feedback, particularly in settings where there are high expectations from parents and stakeholders about student performance.

Furthermore, even when self-assessment practices are implemented, they can occur in ways that encourage students to devalue them or their own evaluations. Many teachers are concerned that sharing assessment control with students through self-assessment will invariably lower standards by potentially allowing students to inflate their self-assessment grades (Ross, 2006). Indeed, over half the primary and secondary school Spanish teachers surveyed by Panadero, Brown, and Courtney (2014) indicated that student self-assessment was not accurate. In light of such concerns, it is not surprising that students in Ross, Rolheiser, and Hogaboam-Gray's (1998) study reported wondering what the point of their self-assessments was when student evaluations were overridden by the teacher's judgments anyway. Unless students can be shifted toward a mastery approach to learning, they may also devalue self-assessment when it does not contribute to their overall marks (Ross et al., 1998).

Hence, when pursuing self-assessment in the classroom, it is important to work with students in ways that encourage all to view assessment as a shared responsibility rather than as the exclusive domain of the teacher or other external assessors. This means that teachers must tell students about the importance of their involvement in assessment and, wherever possible, allow them to have active roles in the setting of tasks and construction of criteria and standards for judging them. In order to shift students toward mastery approaches to learning, teachers must position self-assessment as a useful tool for deeper learning. As Andrade and Brookhart (2016) explain,

> Rather than telling students to peer or self-assess in order to get a better grade, we can explain that seeking feedback from oneself and others is a learning skill that, when honed into a habit, is a hallmark of successful learners.
>
> (p. 304)

As stated earlier, this is in line with an approach that treats self-assessment as a learning process rather than as an evaluative one.

Making Complex Learning Objectives Transparent

Self-assessment practices are diverse, and as will be discussed further in Chapter 4, they range from very simple procedures to ones that require highly complex judgments. For example, it is far easier for students to check their own answers against a list of correct objective responses than it is to use a rubric to evaluate the quality of their work on a complex task. One of the biggest challenges with more complex and intellectually valuable versions of self-assessment, like the use of scripts and rubrics, is that it is far more difficult for educators (let alone students) to come to a shared understanding of what quality looks like for tasks where there are many possible right or high-quality responses (e.g., essays, projects, portfolios). Because teachers often draw on their own implicit, latent, and meta-criteria when assessing, they may disagree on how to apply rubrics to student work (Wyatt-Smith & Klenowski, 2012; Wyatt-Smith, Klenowski, & Gunn, 2010). Indeed, teachers often award grades for student performance without reference to the standards embedded within their work programs or syllabi (Hay & MacDonald, 2008). Hence, students cannot be assumed to understand how to apply external criteria to their own work (Ross et al., 1998).

To alleviate this challenge, it is necessary for teachers to have robust professional discussions about what quality looks like. Such talk allows the development of shared understanding of quality within subjects, grade levels, or departments. This can be done by jointly deconstructing exemplars or by taking part in moderation processes where multiple teachers assess a piece of work to calibrate their judgments (Wyatt-Smith et al., 2010). Standard-setting exercises can also contribute to a deeper sense of criteria and standards.

The next step is to discuss how to communicate these shared expectations with students using language they can understand. Research suggests it is best if teachers co-construct rubrics with students (Andrade, 2013), keeping in mind that key elements valued by the curriculum must be present within these. Although there are no guarantees, at least one study (Newmann, Marks, & Gamoran, 1996) has found that student-made rubrics can be similar to officially mandated rubrics.

Finally, students cannot be expected to assess complex performance without training and support, something we will explore in more detail in Chapter 5. It is vital that students are helped to understand what quality performance looks like via exemplars, clear criteria and standards, and/or checklists. Keep in mind that it is important to show diverse examples of quality work to help students understand how desired attributes can be manifested in different ways. Students also need multiple low-stakes opportunities to practice self-assessing (i.e., comparing their own work to expectations) with opportunities for feedback, not only on their work but also on the credibility of their self-assessments. Such feedback could come from teachers or trusted peers, provided a psychologically safe environment with high trust and interdependence exists.

Creating a Psychologically Safe Environment for Self-Assessment

Although self-assessment can be implemented in ways where the learner has complete privacy (Andrade, 2010), the reality is that in most classrooms there is usually some level of disclosure, whether to the teacher, peers, and/or parents. For example, teachers often look at or ask about self-assessment results and may share these results with parents (Harris & Brown, 2013). Public self-assessments (e.g., Traffic Lights, Thumbs-Up/Thumbs-Down) are conducted in front of classmates, but even more private forms may be the topic of peer discussion or may be viewed when classmates look at one another's work (with or without permission). Hence, it is imperative that students feel that the classroom is a psychologically safe place if they are to reveal honest self-assessments of their work. This is especially necessary if students are likely to reveal that their work is not of the highest or expected standard.

When there is trust, students can feel comfortable disclosing weaknesses to teachers, potentially leading to additional help. As an American student explained in Raider-Roth's (2005) study, self-assessment can lead to very productive student-teacher dialogues: *"You're telling the teacher this and the teacher in turn knows your weaknesses and then you can just express yourself freely"* (p. 596).

Classroom relationships must be strong if teachers expect students to honestly respond to self-assessment activities (Raider-Roth,

2005). Studies have shown that when students fear teacher responses, they purposely provide false self-assessment data to cover for their lack of understanding or problems within their work (Harris & Brown, 2013; see also the following case study for more details). In this case study, self-assessment became an exercise in dishonesty because there was a lack of trust between students and their teacher and peers. Self-assessment requires a culture within the classroom where it is okay to make mistakes and to struggle to understand concepts. Although creating such a culture is easier said than done, for self-assessment to be effective, students must be helped to believe that misunderstandings and mistakes are all part of the learning process (McMillan, 2018) and that disclosing their own perceived lack of understanding in front of teachers and peers is normal and helpful.

Psychological Safety: Case Study

Year 7 teacher Danielle Johnson was trying to implement the Traffic Lights self-assessment practice she had learned about in an assessment for learning workshop. She asked students to rate their understanding of the concept they had learned after each small-group mathematics lesson. When students reported low levels of understanding, she would offer further help. However, after we talked to her students in focus groups, it soon became apparent that some were not being honest within this activity because they were worried about their teacher's opinion (Harris & Brown, 2013, p. 107):

Chelsea: *Because if you put red [in your traffic light], you feel like she might tell us off or something.*

Natasha: *She'll tell us to listen more or something, like we weren't listening.*

Michael: *She always turns it against us if we're not learning.*

Likewise, concerns about peer opinions also led some to produce false self-assessments:

Sally: Yesterday, we were learning to simplify fractions and I couldn't actually understand what she was saying, so I don't actually know how to simplify fractions.

Interviewer: That's okay. Have you told Mrs. Johnson that? Did you put red in your traffic light?

Sally: I did orange.

Interviewer: And why did you do orange?

Sally: Um, Jason was looking at my work and if I did red, he'd think I was dumb, so I just did orange.

Peer expectations may cause students to purposely over- or undervalue their work or to hide misunderstandings (Cowie, 2005; Harris & Brown, 2013; Ross et al., 1998). Raider-Roth (2005) describes these dilemmas as situations where students have to weigh up the benefits of being true to themselves versus considerations about the reactions others might have to their responses. For example, one American student in her study described her self-assessment response as follows:

It is true that I think I'm good at writing paragraphs. I could say that some of my paragraphs aren't as good as they could be and I could write that . . . but the teachers will no doubt talk about it in the room in front of twenty of us, so I'm just gonna write a very short, sweet, true but not totally, answer.

(Raider-Roth, 2005, p. 612)

In situations such as this, in which students do not believe that the full truth, including disclosure of weaknesses and faults in their work, will be well received, self-assessment becomes an exercise in lying or at least in ego protection. Thus, self-assessment loses any potential learning benefit for students and teachers.

Issues around privacy and disclosure are challenging within the context of self-assessment. As Tierney and Koch (2016) identify, students require privacy to learn and develop, something that can be hard to find in classrooms given that teachers are expected to constantly monitor student learning and report it to administrators and families. In the case of self-assessment, if students know that their teachers and potentially their parents will be reading their self-evaluations, they are likely to write such evaluations for this audience. If the teacher/student relationship is problematic, it is highly unlikely that students will admit to gaps in understanding or deficiencies in their work within a self-assessment, even if they are aware of these (Harris & Brown, 2013).

This creates a dilemma for teachers. If they do not look at the student's self-assessment, they will be unable to provide feedback on its accuracy or use such data to modify instruction. However, if they do, knowledge that the self-assessment will be viewed may influence a student's willingness to truthfully self-assess. Because of this issue, some authors (e.g., Andrade, 2010; Andrade & Brown, 2016) suggest that it is best if students are, at least sometimes, allowed to keep their self-assessments entirely private.

However, this need for privacy must be balanced with the need for external feedback on the accuracy of the self-evaluations. Students must, at least sometimes, have the chance to see if their personal evaluations of their work align with curriculum and teacher expectations. Part of the purpose of self-assessment within schools is to teach students to internalize the standards that describe quality work. Hence, it is necessary that teachers know if their students have successfully understood these standards.

Accessing student self-assessments also allows teachers to see the qualities of the student's work from the student's perspective, highlighting what the student values as well as his or her reasoning. Indeed, this is the one type of information that all other types of assessment cannot demonstrate: What does the learner think about his or her own learning and why? As the creators of the work, students will have insights into the processes that contributed to the work and that may prove useful to the teacher. Students may legitimately attend to and value different aspects of the work than those the teacher chooses to focus on. Through this process, the teacher may also discover that the learner has incidentally learned many things other than what was intended (Bourke, 2016).

However, this access comes with the expectation that the teacher will engage meaningfully when students identify problems or weaknesses. We acknowledge that this doesn't always happen. For example, in one New Zealand intermediate school book-work situation we have seen, the student wrote, *"This was extremely hard, and I guessed some of it because I didn't get it"* to which the teacher wrote, *"You did so well at this. Well done!"* This type of teacher response potentially teaches students very quickly not to bother with the complete truth.

Clearly, if there is not an environment of trust (or if relationships are just being established, as at the beginning of a school year), it seems ideal for self-assessments to remain private. However, there are still ways in which students can be given feedback. For simple, objective tasks, correct answers (along with explanations of how to obtain the answers or why they are correct) can be provided to help students evaluate their self-assessments and to understand why their answers are correct or incorrect. For more complex tasks, worked examples or exemplars of different levels of achievement can help students better determine if they have been overly optimistic or pessimistic relative to the grading schema or rubric that the teacher would use. If certain types of technology are available (e.g., clickers or Internet polling programs that allow for anonymous responses), teachers may be able to get instantaneous and potentially anonymous responses to questions they pose in the classroom. Such information about students' perceptions of their own levels of understanding or of the quality of a particular piece of work has the potential to appropriately inform teaching. However, it is important to remember that although self-assessment through polling software can potentially allow students to make judgments (e.g., *My level of understanding is high, medium, or low*), it doesn't require them to justify their self-assessments, which is a much more cognitively challenging and beneficial skill to develop.

As trusting relationships are established, teachers can potentially gain access to student self-assessment data to see how they understand the criteria and standards for quality work. Ideally, teacher observation of self-assessments would include some form of discussion with the student in which reasons for judgments are shared and discrepancies in their evaluations are mediated. Teachers must be aware that there is a potential for conflict between the convergent approach of evaluating student work against formal criteria and the more divergent approach of allowing students to define their own learning and goals (Bourke, 2016; Tan, 2008). However, self-assessment conversations between stakeholders can help create a shared understanding of what should be valued.

Moving Beyond Ego and Minimizing Negative Student Conceptions

Despite the proven benefits of self-assessment and generally positive student conceptions of it (Brown & Harris, 2013), in some classrooms, there may be underlying resistance to these practices. Three issues stand out from the literature.

The first, as mentioned earlier, is the notion that assessment is the sole responsibility of the teacher (Harris & Brown, 2013; Peterson & Irving, 2008; Ross, 2006). Students may ask why the whole exercise is necessary because, as one student told Cowie (2009), *"It's really just telling yourself what you already know"* (p. 93). Particularly if self-assessment practices are repetitive (e.g., frequently completing lengthy templates), students may describe them as boring (Ross et al., 1998).

Additionally, particular student mind-sets can negate self-assessment's positive influence on learning. Returning to the dual-processing model of self-regulation discussed in Chapter 2 (Boekaerts, 1997; Boekaerts & Corno, 2005), students who value well-being goals over growth ones will be less willing to identify faults in their work, as doing so may damage their egos.

There is also a conundrum as to whether self-assessment should contribute to the student's academic grade. Performance-oriented students may view self-assessment as pointless if it does not contribute directly to their summative or total grades. However, if it does, they may be concerned about peers "cheating," or they may be personally motivated to inflate their self-assessments (Ross et al., 1998).

However, apart from these concerns (most of which apply equally to the majority of classroom tasks), self-assessment has some unique challenges to overcome. The first is in getting students to separate themselves (and their egos) from their work. It is important to remind students that self-assessment is not about evaluating themselves as a people but rather about judging, evaluating, and considering the quality of their work or abilities to do the work (Kasanen & Räty, 2002). During self-assessment, if students view their work as an extension of themselves, then self-assessment becomes an exercise in evaluating themselves as people rather than in judging a piece of work that they happened to create. It is clear how tempting it would be for a student to be overly optimistic about work quality if the process is perceived as an exercise in demonstrating or protecting one's own self-esteem and self-regard.

Hence, it is necessary to encourage students, as much as possible, to separate the judgment of their task's quality from any judgments they may make about themselves. Students, particularly academically weaker ones and more novice learners (Brown & Harris, 2013), may need to be encouraged to see identifying weaknesses in their work as a necessary part of learning to think and work like experts. This understanding needs to be embedded within a model of self-assessment where students acknowledge that it is about the work and not about the person.

Self-assessment processes can also be distorted due to cultural or personal traits. In Western societies, it is almost universal that people will be unrealistically optimistic about themselves and their capabilities (Dunning, Heath, & Suls, 2004). Interestingly, optimistic self-assessment is "associated with greater happiness, less depression and anxiety" (Boucher, 2010, p. 304). However, such optimism within Western societies is not universal; girls are more likely to undervalue the quality of their work (Brown & Harris, 2013). Likewise, cultural assumptions and beliefs can also systematically affect the veracity of self-assessments. For example, in some societies (e.g., East Asia cultures), describing oneself as above average is less commonplace, and there is a major emphasis on modesty and humility, whereas in other societies (e.g., Western cultures), being highly positive about oneself is regarded as normal (Boucher, 2010). It is vital for teachers, especially those working in multicultural classrooms, to be aware of how their students' potentially different cultural values may influence self-assessment responses (although we encourage educators not to be overly reliant on cultural or gender stereotypes).

If we want educational improvement to occur as a result of self-assessment, students must first accept that there are areas of potential growth in relation to the work already done. They must have a strong enough sense of self to be able to (a) separate the work from their self-worth and (b) work on the identified deficiencies. In environments where students are encouraged to make and learn from their mistakes, they are less likely to conceal misunderstandings and mistakes during self-assessments. In order to teach learners to create realistic self-assessments, as opposed to falsely inflated or depressed ones, activities that prioritize and reward honesty in self-assessment may help counteract the threats caused by the personality, gender, and cultural traits discussed here.

Improving the Accuracy and Validity of Student Self-Assessments

Accuracy and validity in self-assessment are most usefully understood as the assessment's degree of realism or truthfulness. Hence, the goal of self-assessment is not an inflated positive evaluation, nor is it a negative falsely humble appraisal. The goal is to describe, as accurately as possible using agreed-upon criteria and standards, the quality of the work under consideration. Our assumption is that realism supports appropriate decisions as to what needs to be done next (if anything). Student self-assessments can have significant consequences for the learner if the student acts on a false assessment (e.g., fixes something that was correct the first time around, continues to follow an inappropriate process on future problems). Using a wrong reference point or inappropriate criteria in self-assessment could lead to considerable negative consequences. Consider the student who is ranked in the bottom half of his school's advanced mathematics class who assesses his chances of success at university mathematics as poor because of his relative position in the class. In fact, he would have a high probability of success given that he is in this advanced class. When students use inappropriate reference points, their self-assessments can potentially lead them to inaccurate perceptions of their abilities.

However, how *accuracy* is defined is potentially problematic. As Yan and Brown (2017) note,

> A technical challenge in self-assessment has to do with establishing a valid criterion to judge whether or not a student self-assessment is accurate. While it is conventional to refer to teacher judgments or test scores as a benchmark, it is difficult to know how a *self*-assessment could be classified as *wrong*.
>
> (p. 2)

In other words, if the *self* says this work is good because "*I worked hard on it*," it is difficult without reference to some external authority to say, "*Yes, you worked hard, but you are wrong about how good your work is.*" Interestingly, if the self's perspective can be questioned, then surely the authority of the exemplars, rubrics, scripts, test scores, or teachers can also be questioned. Hence, the external authority has to work somewhat harder to establish its credibility to the self who has unique information about what was done.

Although students may purposely distort their self-assessments for a variety of reasons, as highlighted in the previous two sections, there are also other threats that can sabotage the realism of self-assessment. First, students and teachers may value different aspects of the work. For example, particularly within primary school, presentation, neatness, and length are often valued over content, ideas, organization, or creativity in student writing (even if the latter is valued within the curriculum). If teachers do not focus on the agreed-upon criteria and standards of quality, then students learn from the "hidden" curriculum what really matters and adjust their judgments in accordance with what teachers really prioritize.

Likewise, students can judge their work based on inappropriate criteria (e.g., effort, time spent on a task). For example, when citing what he liked about self-assessment, a school student in Ross et al.'s (1998) study indicated clearly that effort should be taken into account:

> *The teacher only knows so much of how much effort you put into it. She has to look over the whole class. You know personally how hard you worked on it and how much time you worked at home or if you were just goofing off.*

> (p. 470)

Research has shown that even higher education students have requested higher grades because of the effort they expended on the task (Hawe, 2002).

If we assume that alignment of teacher and student judgments based on a curriculum statement or framework is an appropriate measure of accuracy, one of the major issues threatening the likelihood of such agreement is the difference these stakeholders have in their competence. We expect that teachers have a greater, richer, and more sophisticated understanding of what quality looks like and the processes students can use to improve the quality of their work. These skills are known as content knowledge and pedagogical content knowledge, respectively. Based on this greater expertise, we should expect teacher assessments of quality to be more credible than those of novice learners.

This differential in expertise may underpin the concerns students express about their own ability to accurately self-assess (Harris & Brown, 2013; Peterson & Irving, 2008; Ross et al., 1998). Hence, it may be simply unrealistic to expect students, particularly young or novice ones, to have the ability to apply complex criteria to work like an experienced teacher. Brown and Harris (2013) observed that

> lack of competence in a domain (as would be expected in a low progress learner or a beginner) has a dual-handicapping effect; such people are not very good in the domain and, at the same time, are not aware that they are not good in the domain.
>
> (p. 370)

Generally, within the classroom, it is a given that there needs to be alignment between the student's judgment and curricular expectations, meaning some level of monitoring is needed to make sure student judgments are based on the criteria embedded within the curriculum. Once positive and supportive classroom relationships have been established, teachers can potentially cross-mark self-assessments and provide learners with feedback around how they have applied the criteria to their own work, telling the learner, "*Yes, you really do understand this*" or "*Unfortunately, you still misunderstand this part.*" A teacher in one of our studies explained the value of the cross-marking process this way:

> There are students who just don't have a handle on the criteria and will mark it wrongly, but part of that was the point of going through and doing a cross-check. And it's probably quite valuable to find out when students mark something quite wrongly because they obviously don't have a handle on what they're aiming for.
>
> (Harris & Brown, 2013, p. 108)

It is also important to realize that the way self-assessment is set up can encourage students to falsify or make up information. For example, one primary student in our study admitted: "*If she [the teacher] says, 'You guys have to get a bit more detailed for your comments,' sometimes, I just make stuff up*" (Harris & Brown, 2013, p. 106). Although it is potentially important to set some guidelines on length so that students provide responses with sufficient depth, such requirements also mean students have to be helped to generate this level of response so that the final product is quality work.

Getting Students to Act on Self-Assessment Data

One of the biggest challenges relating to all forms of feedback, including that from self-assessment, is getting students to act on it in ways that are adaptive and that promote growth and learning. Like all other feedback situations, self-assessment feedback without action is relatively pointless. Hence, it is essential that students are not only taught to identify what is effective and what is wrong, problematic, or weak about their work but also are helped to develop strategies that will enable them to respond appropriately to the identified issues *and* given time to do so. Just as teachers need to develop pedagogical content knowledge to effectively assess work and determine next learning steps, students must gain some of these skills to maximize their own abilities to conduct and use self-assessment.

It appears particularly important that self-assessment, even if it is conducted at the end of a task, leads to adaptive actions in the future. Ideally, self-assessment is formative (Andrade & Brown, 2016), even if it is conducted at a terminal point in the learning process, because the student should benefit from self-reflection regardless of its timing. Nonetheless, it is important for the teacher to allow students the time and opportunity to continue working on any weaknesses identified in a self-assessment. For example, feedback from a self-assessment conducted at the end of a unit of work may be used to help generate learning targets or goals for the subsequent unit. Alternatively, students may be given the chance to revise their work in light of their self-assessments; this may be more necessary if the work is going to be marked for course grading. This practice of drafting is common in such areas as writing or studio arts. Ultimately, although some forms of self-assessment provide value in helping students improve their work (e.g., when rubrics are interpreted and used), feedback generated when discussing that self-assessment with a peer or a teacher is perhaps most likely to lead to learning and self-regulation. Such discussions increase the probability that self-assessment leads to implementation of the changes identified through the self-assessment process.

Summary

Self-assessment as a classroom practice comes with many complexities that practitioners must be aware of and manage if it is to improve student learning and self-regulation. This chapter has identified six challenges to be addressed, providing some strategies to mitigate potential problems and avoid naively enacted practices.

It is essential to get students to own self-assessment processes. This may require teachers to partially dismantle the teacher/ student power hierarchy common in most classrooms. Students should be empowered to see themselves as potentially competent assessors and feedback providers.

Teachers must also work to make complex learning objectives transparent because students can only assess their progress against criteria and standards that they can visualize and understand. Teachers may be able to use such tools as rubrics, exemplars, and/or checklists to help students better understand the end product of their learning and what quality performance looks like. Additionally, it is important to develop ways for students to deconstruct criteria and standards both on their own and jointly with the teacher and/or classmates.

It is also imperative that teachers create a psychologically safe environment for self-assessment. Research demonstrates that if students do not trust their teachers and/or their peers, they will be unlikely to admit to misunderstandings or faults within their work. Hence, teachers must build a classroom climate where mistakes are considered to be an important part of the learning process.

Students must also be taught to move beyond their egos by emotionally separating their identity from their work. Teachers must be aware of personality traits or cultural values within their students that might undermine the accuracy of their responses (e.g., false humility/modesty vs. egotism). It is vital that students are taught not to view their work as an extension of themselves; otherwise, when they conduct self-assessments, they will also be judging themselves as people, making any negative appraisal potentially damaging to their self-esteem.

Steps must also be taken to maximize the accuracy and validity of self-assessment. Although it is important to provide students with privacy as they begin self-assessing their work, teachers need to offer resources (e.g., worked examples, task exemplars, checklists, clear criteria) to help students calibrate their own judgments, making sure they align with curriculum expectations.

Finally, like any other form of feedback, self-assessment holds little value if it is not drawn on in a strategic way to help the student self-regulate and improve learning. It is recommended that self-assessment is placed within the learning cycle so that students can act immediately on the feedback they have generated to improve their progress on the task. Students should be given time after generating their own feedback to implement the proposed changes. The next chapter goes into more detail about specific classroom self-assessment techniques that can help students produce this useful feedback, identifying strengths and weaknesses within each.

References

Andrade, H. (2010). Students as the definitive source of formative assessment: Academic self-assessment and the self-regulation of learning. In H. L. Andrade & G. J. Cizek (Eds.), *Handbook of formative assessment* (pp. 90–105). New York, NY: Routledge.

Andrade, H. (2013). Classroom assessment in the context of learning theory and research. In J. McMillan (Ed.), *Sage handbook of research in classroom assessment* (pp. 17–34). Thousand Oaks, CA: Sage.

Andrade, H., & Brookhart, S. M. (2016). The role of classroom assessment in supporting self-regulated learning. In D. Laveault & L. Allal (Eds.), *Assessment for learning: Meeting the challenge of implementation* (pp. 293–309). Cham, Switzerland: Springer International.

Andrade, H., & Brown, G. T. L. (2016). Student self-assessment in the classroom. In G. T. L. Brown & L. R. Harris (Eds.), *Handbook of human and social conditions in assessment* (pp. 319–334). New York, NY: Routledge.

Boekaerts, M. (1997). Self-regulated learning: A new concept embraced by researchers, policy makers, educators, teachers, and students. *Learning and Instruction, 7*, 161–186.

Boekaerts, M., & Corno, L. (2005). Self-regulation in the classroom: A perspective on assessment and intervention. *Applied Psychology*, *54*(2), 199–231. doi:10.1111/j.1464-0597.2005.00205.x

Boucher, H. C. (2010). Understanding Western-East Asian differences and similarities in self-enhancement. *Social and Personality Psychology Compass*, *4*(5), 304–317. doi:10.1111/j.1751-9004.2010.00266.x

Bourke, R. (2016). Liberating the learner through self-assessment. *Cambridge Journal of Education*, *46*(1), 97–111. doi:10.1080/0305764X.2015.1015963

Brown, G. T. L., & Harris, L. R. (2013). Student self-assessment. In J. H. McMillan (Ed.), *Sage handbook of research on classroom assessment* (pp. 367–393). Thousand Oaks, CA: Sage.

Brown, G. T. L., & Wang, Z. (2013). Illustrating assessment: How Hong Kong University students conceive of the purposes of assessment. *Studies in Higher Education*, *38*(7), 1037–1057. doi:10.1080/03075079.2011.616955

Cowie, B. (2005). Pupil commentary on assessment for learning. *Curriculum Journal*, *16*(2), 137–151.

Cowie, B. (2009). My teacher and my friends help me learn: Student perspectives and experiences of classroom assessment. In D. M. McInerney, G. T. L. Brown, & G. A. D. Liem (Eds.), *Student perspectives on assessment: What students can tell us about assessment for learning* (pp. 85–105). Charlotte, NC: Information Age.

Dunning, D., Heath, C., & Suls, J. M. (2004). Flawed self-assessment: Implications for health, education, and the workplace. *Psychological Science in the Public Interest*, *5*(3), 69–106.

Harris, L. R., & Brown, G. T. L. (2013). Opportunities and obstacles to consider when using peer- and self-assessment to improve student learning: Case studies into teachers' implementation. *Teaching and Teacher Education*, *36*, 101–111. doi:10.1016/j.tate.2013.07.008

Hawe, E. M. (2002). Assessment in a pre-service teacher education programme: The rhetoric and the practice of standards-based assessment. *Asia-Pacific Journal of Teacher Education*, *30*(1), 93–106.

Hay, P. J., & Macdonald, D. (2008). (Mis)appropriations of criteria and standards-referenced assessment in a performance-based subject. *Assessment in Education: Principles, Policy & Practice*, *15*(2), 153–168.

Kasanen, K., & Räty, H. (2002). "You be sure now to be honest in your assessment": Teaching and learning self-assessment. *Social Psychology of Education*, *5*(4), 313–328. doi:10.1023/A:1020993427849

McMillan, J. H. (2018). *Using students' assessment mistakes and learning deficits to enhance motivation and learning*. New York, NY: Routledge.

Mehan, H. (1979). *Learning lessons: Social organization in the classroom*. Cambridge, MA: Harvard University Press.

Newmann, F. M., Marks, H. M., & Gamoran, A. (1996). Authentic pedagogy and student performance. *American Journal of Education*, *104*(4), 280–312. doi:10.1086/444136

Nichols, S. L., & Berliner, D. C. (2007). *Collateral damage: How high-stakes testing corrupts America's schools*. Cambridge, MA: Harvard Education Press.

Nichols, S. L., & Harris, L. R. (2016). Accountability assessment's effects on teachers and schools. In G. T. L. Brown & L. R. Harris (Eds.), *Handbook of human and social conditions in assessment* (pp. 40–56). New York, NY: Routledge.

Panadero, E., Brown, G. T. L., & Courtney, M. G. (2014). Teachers' reasons for using self-assessment: A survey self-report of Spanish teachers. *Assessment in Education: Principles, Policy and Practice*, *21*(4), 365–383. doi:10.1080/0969594X.2014.919247

Peterson, E. R., & Irving, S. E. (2008). Secondary school students' conceptions of assessment and feedback. *Learning and Instruction*, *18*(3), 238–250.

Raider-Roth, M. B. (2005). Trusting what you know: Negotiating the relational context of classroom life. *Teachers College Record*, *107*(4), 587–628.

Reay, D., & Wiliam, D. (1999). "I'll be a nothing": Structure, agency and the construction of identity through assessment. *British Educational Research Journal*, *25*(3), 343–354.

Remesal, A. (2009). Accessing primary pupils' conceptions of daily classroom assessment practices. In D. M. McInerney, G. T. L. Brown, & G. A. D. Liem (Eds.), *Student perspectives on assessment: What students can tell us about assessment for learning* (pp. 25–51). Charlotte, NC: Information Age.

Ross, J. A. (2006). The reliability, validity, and utility of self-assessment. *Practical Assessment, Research, and Evaluation*, *11*(10), 1–13.

Ross, J. A., Rolheiser, C., & Hogaboam-Gray, A. (1998). Skills training versus action research in-service: Impact on student attitudes to self-evaluation. *Teaching and Teacher Education*, *14*(5), 463–477.

Sadler, P. M., & Good, E. (2006). The impact of self- and peer-grading on student learning. *Educational Assessment*, *11*(1), 1–31.

Sinnema, C., & Aitken, G. (2012). *Effective pedagogy in social sciences* (Vol. 23). Brussels, Belgium: UNESCO International Bureau of Education and the Academy of Education.

Tan, K. H. (2008). Qualitatively different ways of experiencing student self-assessment. *Higher Education Research & Development, 27*(1), 15–29.

Tierney, R. D., & Koch, M. J. (2016). Privacy in classroom assessment. In G. T. L. Brown & L. R. Harris (Eds.), *Handbook of human and social conditions in assessment* (pp. 267–283). New York, NY: Routledge.

Tomlinson, C. A., & Moon, T. R. (2013). Differentiation and classroom assessment. In J. H. McMillan (Ed.), *Sage handbook of research on classroom assessment* (pp. 415–430). Thousand Oaks, CA: Sage.

Torrance, H., & Pryor, J. (1998). *Investigating formative assessment: Teaching, learning and assessment in the classroom.* Buckingham, England: Open University Press.

Wheelock, A., Bebell, D., & Haney, W. (2000). What can student drawings tell us about high-stakes testing in Massachusetts? *Teachers College Record* (ID Number: 10634).

Wyatt-Smith, C., & Klenowski, V. (2012). Explicit, latent and meta-criteria: Types of criteria at play in professional judgment practice. *Assessment in Education: Principles, Policy & Practice, 20*(1), 35–52. doi:10.1080/0969594x.2012.725030

Wyatt-Smith, C., Klenowski, V., & Gunn, S. (2010). The centrality of teachers' judgment practice in assessment: A study of standards in moderation. *Assessment in Education: Principles, Policy & Practice, 17*(1), 59–75. doi:10.1080/09695940903565610

Yan, Z., & Brown, G. T. L. (2017). A cyclical self-assessment process: Towards a model of how students engage in self-assessment. *Assessment & Evaluation in Higher Education, 42*(8), 1247–1262. doi:10.1080/02602938.2016.1260091

4

Unpacking Common Self-Assessment Practices

Although self-assessment can lead to improved student self-regulation and learning, the challenges highlighted in Chapter 3 underscore the importance of careful planning and implementation. In this chapter, we differentiate between formal self-assessment processes that teachers instigate and informal self-assessment that students may do on a daily basis within the classroom without any kind of prompting (Yan & Brown, 2017). Although the latter is to be encouraged, this chapter focuses on how teachers can effectively set up varying kinds of self-assessment practices within their classrooms.

Clearly, teachers need to carefully consider which self-assessment technique they will use with their students, why they will use this technique (as opposed to others or none at all), and how implementation will take place. The goal of this chapter is to help readers better understand the purposes for and benefits of many common self-assessment techniques employed in classrooms to better inform decision making around self-assessment.

Implementation Considerations: The Devil Is in the Details

As noted in our definition of self-assessment in Chapter 1, we include a diverse range of practices under the banner of self-assessment. Nonetheless, we do not argue that all practices have equal potential to contribute to student self-regulation and learning. Evidence suggests that practices only improve self-regulation "provided such self-evaluation involves deep engagement with the processes affiliated with self-regulation (i.e., goal setting, self-monitoring, and evaluation against valid, objective standards)" (Brown & Harris, 2013, p. 386). Although there are certainly some types of self-assessment practices that are more aligned with the processes of self-regulation than others, implementation matters.

It may seem obvious that how practices are executed within the classroom will have a significant impact on their effectiveness: "It is the implementation and complexity of the self-assessment, more so than the type, which generates the positive effects" (Brown & Harris, 2013, p. 383). For example, in a study where we examined the content of students' written self-assessment comments, we found significant variation in the quality of student comments (Harris, Brown, & Harnett, 2015). Consider the potential learning value of each of the following student self-assessment comments (Harris et al., 2015, p. 272):

- "*I talked a lot on* [sic] *this session and it was fun.*"
- "*I need to work on finding information in texts and understanding what I am reading.*"

Clearly, the second has significantly more value for learning than the first, even though both students had been asked to write a self-assessment comment about their performance on a specific task. Although age may be a factor (the first comment was from a New Zealand Year 6 student, while the second comment was from a Year 10 student), the second student also had access to detailed criteria and standards when making his self-assessment, which likely helped him focus on evaluating specific characteristics of his work.

Hence, as you consider using the self-assessment practices discussed in the subsequent sections, in addition to considerations about what type might be most effective for your purposes, we encourage you to think carefully about the details within implementation, regardless of what technique you select. It is helpful to consider the following questions:

- What success criteria and standards are you going to share (or co-construct) with your students to help them understand the features of quality work prior to making any self-assessment?
- How are you going to help them understand how to apply these to their own work during self-assessment?
- What strategies will you have in place to help mitigate the potential threats to self-assessment described in the previous chapter?

Self-Assessment Practices

A range of self-assessment techniques that are often used with primary, secondary, and sometimes tertiary students are introduced. These include the following:

- Estimating future performance
- Simple self-ratings
- Self-marking
- Self-assessment templates and checklists
- Self-assessment scripts
- Rubric-guided self-assessment

Each practice will be described, along with some of its strengths and limitations. After these have been shared, we will provide some suggestions as to how you might move students developmentally through these practices to help them become competent self-assessors, along with considerations about how technology may impact self-assessment now and in the future.

Estimating Future Performance

Within this practice, often referred to as judgment of learning, students are asked to predict how they will perform on an upcoming task (usually a test), drawing on their analysis of how effectively they have learned the material (Baars, Vink, van Gog, de Bruin, & Paas, 2014; Nelson & Narens, 1990). For example, students might be asked to consider how well they have learned their spelling words for the week and predict how many words they will get correct on an upcoming spelling quiz. Hattie (2009) has shown that when students are asked to predict their performance, there is a large gain in achievement, so being able to do this appears to be highly productive.

Drawing on terms from the self-regulation literature, this kind of self-assessment occurs within the forethought or planning phase of the particular task (the spelling quiz), although the learning of the words may have already occurred. Estimating performance like this is believed to help students in several ways (Meyer, McClure, Walkey, Weir, & McKenzie, 2009):

1. It gets students to review their learning and to judge how proficient they have become (i.e., *I have studied hard this week and know all the words and will get ten out of ten; I am not confident, as I have found these ones difficult, and think I will get six out of ten; I got six out of ten last week. This week's words are harder, so I think I will get five out of ten*).
2. This type of self-assessment allows students to compare their own estimates with their actual performance in a clear and objective way, providing feedback as to their actual competence and as to the accuracy and realism of their self-assessments.
3. This self-assessment can be done privately; there is no need to share the self-assessment with their teacher or peers. Students just need to record or remember their predictions.
4. For some, this judgment of learning may help motivate them to invest greater effort (*I predicted I would do well, so I need to focus and make that happen*). However, there is always the risk that some students will aim for "just enough" instead of

their best, undermining the importance of challenging goals in ensuring high-quality learning.

Although there are clear positives related to judgment of learning (e.g., it allows for student privacy, students can easily measure their predictions against actual outcomes), there are limitations as well. First, it is most effectively used to predict performance on tests that can be scored objectively. Such assessments often focus on reasonably simple knowledge and generally require relatively basic cognitive processes, such as recall (e.g., mathematics basic facts, spelling, vocabulary or terminology). Although accuracy may be hoped for given the concrete and objective nature of this kind of self-assessment, it is important to realize that young children have difficulty in making realistic estimations, even when they have access to clear feedback about their actual performance (Powel & Gray, 1995).

The more complex the performance expected on the assessment, the more difficult it is to predict one's performance accurately. This is particularly the case if the test samples from a large body of knowledge and skills (e.g., *What score will you get on the end-of-year examination of everything you were taught this year in mathematics?*). In such assessments, a large body of work is sampled, and there is a greater likelihood that students will not be able to predict accurately what material will be covered on the examination, making it impossible to judge beforehand how well that material has been learned. With this much uncertainty, students are less likely to accurately predict their performance. The accuracy of their judgment of learning would also be complicated if the examination score was weighted according to item difficulty (e.g., using item response theory) rather than a simple sum of items scored correctly (see Brown, 2018 for more details on this issue).

Second, although this practice relates to self-regulation in that students' predictions form self-constructed learning targets, it does not ask students to tap into deeper metacognitive strategies. Students are not required to evaluate why their performance was good or poor or to give any kind of feedback to themselves about how to do better next time. Hence, judgment of learning tasks are unlikely to get students to engage deeply with learning goals.

Limitations notwithstanding, judgment of learning has a place within self-assessment practices. We suggest that it be used with novice students who have not had much previous experience in self-assessing their work. Its strength is that it can objectively reinforce realism in estimations of capability. If teachers view it as a way to train students to reflect on the accuracy of their judgments in self-assessment, it may be a useful tool for teaching children to be realistic in their self-assessments. This would be strengthened if the teacher engages in conversations with students afterward, asking them to consider why their predictions were or were not accurate and what they could do next time to make their predictions more accurate and to improve their performance. The goal here is not to get students to reduce their targets but rather to increase their efforts to reach those targets.

Simple Self-Ratings

Another fairly simple self-assessment technique is to ask students to rate their levels of understanding or their perceptions about the quality of their work using symbols or gestures. An example of this is the Traffic Lights technique, popularized by the Assessment Reform Group in the United Kingdom (Black, Harrison, Lee, Marshall, & Wiliam, 2003; Leahy, Lyon, Thompson, & Wiliam, 2005). Within assessment for learning, it is used primarily during the performance phase as students are doing the work (because teachers use it to check that students understand the material currently being taught). However, it can also be used during the self-reflection phase while students are evaluating and reflecting on their work. During this activity, the teacher asks the students to self-assess their levels of understanding in relation to a learning goal. In Traffic Lights, the conventional colors of the traffic light are used to indicate a perceived level of progress. Red means the student doesn't understand or hasn't achieved the goal, yellow means the student partially understands but still has some questions or is partway toward achieving the goal, and green indicates full understanding or having achieved this goal. A particular strength of this practice is that teachers can quickly see which and how many students admit to confusion or lack of understanding and respond promptly. As Black et al. (2003) note, "because the response to their needs is immediate, students begin to realize that revealing their problems is worthwhile, as the focus of the teaching is to improve learning rather than to compare one student with another" (p. 52). A variation on this is Thumbs-Up/Thumbs-Down where students indicate with this simple hand gesture whether they have understood the lesson or have achieved the goal in question.

In these simple self-ratings, with the raising of traffic light cards or a showing of thumbs, student responses are publically visible to the teacher (and classmates). A more private version would be to use clickers (i.e., small handheld devices that allow students to respond electronically). These data are usually displayed in aggregate form to the class and used by the teacher to discuss more common difficulties or issues without identifying a specific person reporting the problem.

There are also other simple rating systems students can use to indicate the self-assessment of their own work. For example, students may be asked to draw or color in a smiley face (e.g., happy ☺, neutral ☺, sad ☹) that best matches how well a task has been done or understood. Another variation is to ask students to highlight aspects of their work that they think are good (color one, green), okay (color two, yellow), and could improve (color three, red). Usually, students are asked to self-assess this way on their own daily book work or assignment drafts so that these responses would be seen only by the teacher or parents. With these practices, students may also be asked to write a short explanation for their ratings and suggest what they might do next to continue to improve. Adding this extra explanatory step is highly beneficial for learners, as it forces them to justify their judgment and consider its implications for their next learning steps.

One obvious strength of these practices is that because of their simplicity, these types of self-assessments can potentially provide an entry point for students who have not previously been asked to evaluate their own learning or work. Indeed, the relative simplicity of the rating scale means that approximate judgments (rather than precise measurements) are being requested, a much easier beginning point for novices. Additionally, if students are asked to focus on a specific learning intention or criterion when making their judgments, this can potentially help students to monitor their understanding of what is being learned and to stay focused on the learning goal instead of resorting to a more global assessment of their own ego or self-worth. Practices like Traffic Lights and Thumbs-Up/Thumbs-Down can provide the teacher with rapid feedback on student understanding; when a teacher sees a sea of red traffic lights, it is a clear indication that a change in teaching or activity is needed.

Despite the potential benefits listed in the previous subsection, there are limitations. First, public forms of self-assessment like Traffic Lights and Thumbs-Up/Thumbs-Down may motivate some students to respond dishonestly for ego-protective purposes (Cowie, 2009; Harris & Brown, 2013). Students may be reluctant to show a red traffic light, even though they know they do not understand the concept being taught if they don't want to appear 'stupid' in front of their peers or risk teacher disapproval (Harris & Brown, 2013). Hence, a classroom environment that encourages and rewards honesty, mutual trust, and respect is essential. Teachers considering these practices may want to adopt more private alternatives (e.g., asking students to draw traffic lights in their workbooks that will be viewed only by the teacher or holding their thumbs close to their chests and covering them up with the other hand so only the teacher can see; Brookhart, 2016). Technology, such as clickers or polling applications (e.g., Socrative or Verso; Rotsaert, Panadero, Schellens, & Raes, 2017), may also help provide students with more privacy.

Another issue is that often these relatively simple forms of self-assessment are not always clearly anchored in explicit success criteria and standards for students to use when making their self-evaluations. Instead, they require students to express a sense of learning or perception of understanding. This perception can be wrong if students use inappropriate standards as a basis for their self-assessments (e.g., effort, comparison with the work of peers). For these kinds of practices to be useful for self-regulation and learning, students must have a fairly clear concept of what it is that they are supposed to have learned or been able to do in order to judge whether they have or have not successfully mastered the knowledge or accomplished the task.

Furthermore, the teacher and the students must have a common understanding as to what the ratings (e.g., red, yellow, and green; thumbs-up or thumbs-down) mean in relation to the learning goals. Otherwise, the varying subjective standards that individuals have around what it means to be happy with their work will distort the meaning of the self-assessment. Asking students to explain or defend their self-assessments either orally or in writing will provide insights as to what each student thinks the rating means and encourage students to think deeply as to why they rated their work or comprehension as they did.

Self-Marking

Another relatively common practice that falls under the broad banner of self-assessment is self-marking, at times referred to as self-grading within particular jurisdictions. We use the term self-marking to refer to situations where students correct their answers with an objective answer key (e.g., math problems with one single correct answer, words that can be spelled correctly in only one way, multiple-choice or true/false items). This is different from the process of evaluating one's own work against a rubric that often involves some subjective element in assigning a rubric score. Correct answers may be provided in different ways; for example, they may be called out by the teacher, found in the back of a textbook, or provided in the form of an answer key. Self-marking occurs during the self-reflection phase when students are evaluating and reflecting on their work. It is designed to get students to check their work for accuracy, allowing them to participate in a very basic form of evaluation (*Did I get the answer correct?*) and offering them the opportunity to practice realism and honesty in their scoring.

However, there are ways to maximize student benefit from self-marking activities. Some subjects (e.g., mathematics) depend on sequences or steps that need to be correctly completed to arrive at the right response. For this type of learning, a marking key that provides the correct steps, as well as the final answer, allows students to evaluate their own work against both the final result and the steps used to arrive at the answer. This approach, based on research around worked examples (Sweller, 2006), is highly recommended. Instead of just marking that they got the right answer, students can be asked to see how closely their own working compares to the model answer and indicate how their work is similar and different. Additional self-reflection is triggered if students are required to give explanations for any discrepancies in their work compared to the answer key. It may be that the student has used an alternative legitimate process to get the correct answer that the teacher had not anticipated. Adding these sequences or steps can increase the cognitive challenge within self-marking.

For another way to improve the learning value of self-marking, consider the example Black et al. (2003) share in their book:

> In a Spanish classroom, a teacher had collected in letters that the students had written to pen-friends and had underlined each error. She then gave students a grid which listed such common errors as adjective–noun agreement, incorrect definite article and tense and each student had to classify their errors using tally marks. They did this on three occasions. After the third piece of work had been marked in this way, each student had to decide the type of errors they were making most often, set themselves targets for improvement and then identify a "buddy" in the classroom who had few of these types of errors to help them improve.
>
> (p. 73)

Here students had to first self-grade (i.e., identifying what type of error the teacher had underlined in their work) and then deduce for themselves, using patterns in their own data, what their biggest weaknesses were. They were also provided a strategy (i.e., team up with a peer who is good at this) to help them overcome their problems in this area. Hence, in this implementation, the self-marking was only the first step in a pedagogical (as opposed to an evaluative) process designed to get students to actively self-regulate to redress a weakness.

However, improvement will come only if students are willing to use data gained from self-marking to guide their future efforts. Students must be encouraged to utilize the feedback gained from self-marking activities and to view this process as an exercise in identifying what they got wrong so that they can work on fixing it. Survey studies indicate that students who have this type of adaptive, formative, and self-regulating mind-set about assessment and feedback do better than those who reject feedback (Brown, Peterson, & Irving, 2009; Brown, Peterson, & Yao, 2016).

The logic behind this practice is that if students correct their work themselves, they will be forced to identify which individual items were correct and incorrect and be more aware of their own successes and failures. When teachers mark an activity or quiz, it is easy for the student to just focus on the total score and to not look at which questions or items were answered correctly or incorrectly. Without engaging with their mistakes, it is unlikely that they will focus on their areas of weakness, allowing them to achieve mastery.

Sadler and Good (2006) argued that self-marking is beneficial for two reasons. First, it will save the teacher time and speed up the feedback process. A major benefit is that students can get rapid feedback on the quality of their efforts instead of having to wait for the teacher to correct the work.

Second, it can help students to (a) engage more deeply with their responses and the reasons their answers are correct or incorrect, (b) understand or demystify tests by allowing them to learn how they are assessed, (c) become more aware of their strengths and limitations, (d) become better prepared for future education and work situations, and (e) develop more positive attitudes toward tests by allowing students to see them as a source of useful learning feedback.

Sadler and Good (2006) found that when students marked their own work, their scores when they retook the same test rose (as compared to students who had marked their peers' tests). This suggests that having to mark each and every item on their own tests (rather than someone else's) helped students identify problems in their own understanding and allowed them to address these before the next administration of the same test. Although marking a classmate's test is a common strategy for reducing cheating, this study suggests that there may be greater learning benefit if students are trusted to mark their own tests.

Self-marking can also encourage accuracy in marking, although in practice, students may choose to not be accurate if they think the teacher will not be cross-checking their responses (Harris & Brown, 2013) or if they feel they need to artificially inflate their performance due to self-, peer, or parent expectations (Harris, Brown, & Dargusch, 2018). However, knowing that marking will be checked can encourage students to act in academically honest ways (Murdock, Stephens, & Groteweil, 2016).

Unfortunately, self-marking is quite limited in its scope and complexity because it works most effectively with objective answers. As Dinsmore and Wilson (2016) note, selected response items can be problematic for the development of self-regulated learning as they

> may limit participants' ability to use feedback to self-assess their own learning because if assessment, and thereby knowledge, is in a highly structured form, there may be no need for a student to reflect on his or her own thinking or behavior; rather, the student can just adopt the structured knowledge as presented in the assessment.
>
> (p. 159)

Additionally, an objective answer key normally does not provide explanations for why the answer is correct or why incorrect answers are wrong. Hence, students may be unable to get the explanatory or corrective feedback they need to learn from the process (e.g., they are not following a common spelling rule, they forgot a step in the mathematical process), which a teacher might have given if he or she had marked it. Hence, although this strategy is worth pursuing some of the time, it is advised that teachers do periodically perform this task so that students receive this deeper level of feedback.

Self-Assessment Templates and Checklists

To support the global assessment for learning movement, a growing number of books have been written with relatively generic templates and prompts that teachers can use to help implement popular formative assessment practices within the classroom (e.g., Clarke, 2001, 2005; Clarke, Timperley, & Hattie, 2003). Teachers may also provide their students with such tools as checklists to use for self-assessment, either generic or ones they may have specifically designed for the task.

Clearly, the kinds of self-assessment sheets that we are grouping together in this category are actually quite diverse. Although it is impossible to review all the permutations and combinations of these, we will discuss checklists, a simple common template (Two Stars and a Wish), and a more complex template (Fletcher, 2016) to highlight similarities and differences.

Checklists

Checklists are a very common tool teachers use to help students evaluate their own work, usually before it is submitted for comment and/or grading. Often checklists may appear on or alongside assessment task instructions. Unfortunately, many checklists focus more on completeness and simple structural aspects (e.g., *Do you have a title page? Subheadings?*) rather than on deeper features of the work (e.g., *Have you created a three-dimensional character? Are the hypotheses you developed for your experiment specific and testable?*). Additionally, they do not usually ask students to evaluate the quality of the aspects present. For example, if the student has scrawled a title on a piece of paper, he or she may be able to tick *yes* for having a title page, despite it being of poor quality.

Although checklists can be a helpful way to remind learners of key aspects and structures that should be present within their work, in most instances, there are fairly minimal opportunities for reflection. They may allow learners to identify what is missing, but they seldom encourage students to gain a deep understanding as to why all the items on the checklist are required (it is just assumed that they are necessary), nor do they offer suggestions about how best to recover any missing items. It is perhaps for this reason that Panadero, Alonso-Tapias, and Huertas (2012) consider scripts (discussed in the next section) to be a different entity, despite having features similar to a checklist. Hence, it is important that checklists are also accompanied by rich dialogue both with teachers and with classmates about why items on the checklist are important and how to go about improving them.

Two Stars and a Wish

There are also many generic templates on the market that teachers may use with students to help them self-assess. One popular template is the Two Stars and a Wish approach, usually implemented in the self-reflection phase to help students evaluate their work. Although used for self-assessment, this basic format can also be used for teacher or peer feedback (Webb & Jones, 2009). Here students are asked to identify two positive aspects of their own work, ideally in relation to the agreed-upon success criteria. Then, they create a wish, which is something they hope to improve on or do better next time. This particular strategy tries to tap into positive student affect by getting them to focus primarily on their successes. Its major strength is that it asks students to identify one area for improvement, potentially providing a next learning step.

The challenge with this particular template (and many similar templates) is that it is often implemented in quite simplistic ways. For example, if students are not strongly encouraged to use success criteria and standards for quality work to identify the strengths, they are perhaps unlikely to attend to the features valued within the curriculum when evaluating their work. Instead, they are likely to select random aspects that they personally liked (but that may not be academically relevant). It is worth remembering that adults also have a tendency to be highly subjective in their self-evaluations (Dunning, Heath, & Suls, 2004). Additionally, the template itself does not require students to make any kind of justification for their decisions. Why did they award particular features with stars? Self-regulation literature makes it clear that the process of justification is where many metacognitive processes are activated.

Finally, although it is positive that a wish is included, offering a direction for future progress, unless students are actively encouraged to work toward this goal and are provided with

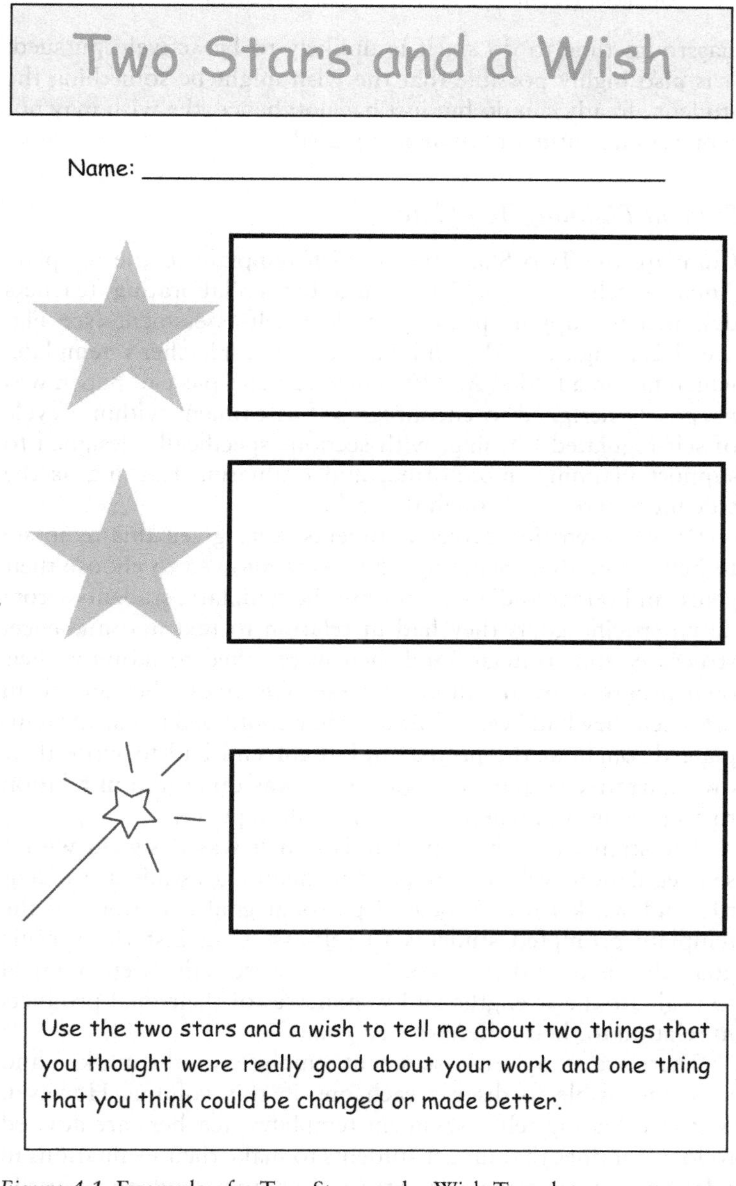

Two Stars and a Wish

Name: _____

Use the two stars and a wish to tell me about two things that you thought were really good about your work and one thing that you think could be changed or made better.

Figure 4.1 Example of a Two Stars and a Wish Template
Source: Assessment for Learning Resources, 2011, p. 1.

classroom time to do so, it is unlikely to be actively pursued. It is also highly possible that the wish might be something the student already can do but just has not; hence, the wish may not represent a legitimate, challenging goal.

Student Planning Template

Compare the Two Stars and a Wish template to the template Anna Fletcher (2016, 2017) and her collaborating teachers designed to support primary student self-assessment (see Figure 4.2a, Figure 4.2b, and Figure 4.2c). Fletcher's template, which fits on a folded A3 (29.7cm × 42.0cm) piece of paper, was purposely designed to encourage self-assessment within a cycle of self-regulated learning, with sections specifically designed to support planning, monitoring, and evaluating learning as the student progresses through the task.

During a writing project, students were given this template to help guide their planning (they were allowed to choose their genre and target audience). Within the template, students wrote down specific goals they had in relation to text and audience, structure, and strategies and then were asked to monitor their own progress toward meeting these objectives, checking them off when they had been achieved. They continued to use the template throughout the project and at the end had to write their own narrative comments about what was done well in relation to their goals and where they could still improve.

The strength of this template is that it was designed with a self-regulation cycle in mind, and it encourages students to identify and work toward focused personal goals. Sections of the template prompted students to self-assess against the specific goals they had set themselves, and they were actively encouraged to evaluate the strengths and weaknesses of their final products in relation to their criteria-based goals.

There are many self-assessment templates on the market, and it is impossible to discuss each one in this volume. However, when evaluating self-assessment templates, teachers are advised to look for ones that (a) get students to make their evaluations in relation to specific goals or criteria, (b) require students to justify

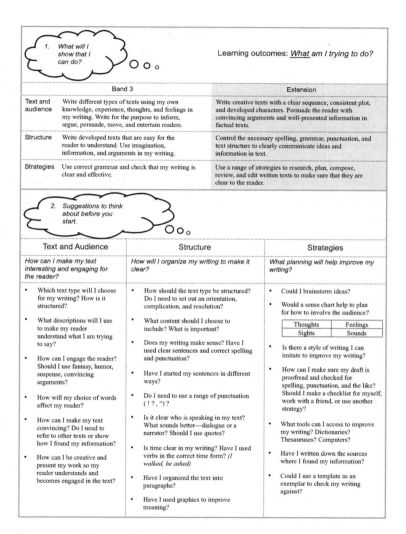

	Band 3	Extension
Text and audience	Write different types of texts using my own knowledge, experience, thoughts, and feelings in my writing. Write for the purpose to inform, argue, persuade, move, and entertain readers.	Write creative texts with a clear sequence, consistent plot, and developed characters. Persuade the reader with convincing arguments and well-presented information in factual texts.
Structure	Write developed texts that are easy for the reader to understand. Use imagination, information, and arguments in my writing.	Control the necessary spelling, grammar, punctuation, and text structure to clearly communicate ideas and information in text.
Strategies	Use correct grammar and check that my writing is clear and effective.	Use a range of strategies to research, plan, compose, review, and edit written texts to make sure that they are clear to the reader.

1. What will I show that I can do?

Learning outcomes: _What am I trying to do?_

2. Suggestions to think about before you start.

Text and Audience	Structure	Strategies
How can I make my text interesting and engaging for the reader?	*How will I organize my writing to make it clear?*	*What planning will help improve my writing?*
• Which text type will I choose for my writing? How is it structured?	• How should the text type be structured? Do I need to set out an orientation, complication, and resolution?	• Could I brainstorm ideas?
• What descriptions will I use to make my reader understand what I am trying to say?	• What content should I choose to include? What is important?	• Would a sense chart help to plan for how to involve the audience?
• How can I engage the reader? Should I use fantasy, humor, suspense, convincing arguments?	• Does my writing make sense? Have I used clear sentences and correct spelling and punctuation?	Thoughts / Feelings / Sights / Sounds
• How will my choice of words affect my reader?	• Have I started my sentences in different ways?	• Is there a style of writing I can imitate to improve my writing?
• How can I make my text convincing? Do I need to refer to other texts or show how I found my information?	• Do I need to use a range of punctuation (! ? , ")?	• How can I make sure my draft is proofread and checked for spelling, punctuation, and the like? Should I make a checklist for myself, work with a friend, or use another strategy?
• How can I be creative and present my work so my reader understands and becomes engaged in the text?	• Is it clear who is speaking in my text? What sounds better—dialogue or a narrator? Should I use quotes?	• What tools can I access to improve my writing? Dictionaries? Thesauruses? Computers?
	• Is time clear in my writing? Have I used verbs in the correct time form? *(I walked, he asked)*	• Have I written down the sources where I found my information?
	• Have I organized the text into paragraphs?	• Could I use a template as an exemplar to check my writing against?
	• Have I used graphics to improve meaning?	

Figure 4.2a Planning Template Part 1
Source: Fletcher, 2016, p. 18.

Text type: *What sort of text will I write?*

3. Think about this as you start planning your work.

Narrative	Explanation	Recount	Report
Poetry	Procedure	Other:_____	

Audience: *Who is the text meant to engage?*

Children	Teenagers	Parents	Teachers
People in Darwin	People in power	Other:_____	

4. Check off as you work.

Assessment checklist: *These are the things I will focus on*

Text and Audience:	My progress
Structure:	
Strategies:	

Figure 4.2b Planning Template Part 2
Source: Fletcher, 2016, p. 19.

Reflection: *Why have I chosen to show my work in this way?*

....
....
_____
_____
....
_____
....
_____
....
_____
....

Self-assessment:

5. At the end, think back.

How did I improve my writing skills? ☆☆☆☆☆

How would I rate my finished work? ☆☆☆☆☆

What did I do the best?

....
_____
....
_____

What can I improve?

....
_____
....
_____

Teacher's feedback:

Figure 4.2c Planning Template Part 3
Source: Fletcher, 2016, p. 20.

their judgments, and (c) ask students to identify areas for future improvement and specify how this might be accomplished.

Self-Assessment Scripts

Another potential self-assessment technique is the use of scripts. Panadero, Jonsson, and Strijbos (2016) explain that a

> script is a list of specific questions, structured in steps that model how an expert in the field would approach a complex task from beginning to end. Scripts can be used as a way to scaffold students' strategies and thinking when solving complex tasks.
>
> (p. 317)

A script can not only be used to guide processes (i.e., encourage students to take similar steps and to ask themselves similar questions as those of an expert), but also to provide students with a way to evaluate their processes, linking to all phases of the self-regulation cycle.

Scripts have many similarities to a checklist, to the point where some scholars argue that they are the same, with different terminology being used due to the fact that scripts have developed from research on scaffolding, whereas checklists are based on work from the field of classroom assessment (Andrade, in press). However, Panadero (personal communication, January 10, 2017) highlights what he sees as key differences. He argues that scripts have grown out of cognitive psychology, particularly the subfield of metacognition, and are closely related to cues and prompts, with a particular focus on process (e.g., *Have I followed this approach?*). In contrast, he views checklists as more associated with the field of education and notes that they tend to focus student attention on specific required outcome aspects that should be present within the final product (*Have I included X?*). Hence, Panadero argues that scripts encourage students to be more metacognitively aware and to reflect on process more than checklists do. In a sense, a script could be viewed as a type of worked example framework (Sweller, 2006). It provides guiding questions that encourage students to go through the processes experts are expected to follow but without demonstrating their actual steps.

For example, consider the script Panadero et al. (2012) developed with collaborating teachers to help students analyze landscapes as part of a high school geography task (see Figure 4.3). This script takes the student through the process an expert would adopt when orienting to and analyzing a landscape. Although some questions ask students to identify key features, particularly within the Interpretation and Classification section, students are expected to use far more probing questions (e.g., *Why do I think that way?*).

One of the major strengths of scripts as a form of self-assessment is that they have the potential to cue learners to key task-specific learning processes. They can help scaffold students to work through complex tasks and encourage them to reflect on and justify decisions while in the process of completing the task. They can also be designed in ways that move students through a self-regulation cycle. Panadero et al.'s (2012) example includes prompts that help students orient to the task, but also ones that help them to reflect on their learning process (i.e., *Has this script helped me to do the landscape analysis?*)

A further strength is that scripts are process oriented, allowing students to reflect on their learning process without anchoring this reflection in a grading or scoring approach. Panadero et al. (2012) found that use of scripts actually led to higher self-regulation than rubrics, perhaps because scripts kept students focused on the learning and the task rather than on grades or scores. Taking away students' ability to score work also likely helps discourage a min-max approach (Covington & Teel, 1996), where students work strategically to get the maximum amount of points for the minimum amount of effort.

However, there are also some potential challenges. Panadero et al.'s (2012) work indicates that students may find this approach more challenging than many of the practices described previously within the chapter (including rubrics), perhaps because reflecting on process is more abstract and difficult for many students. It is potentially difficult to take on the kinds of complex questions

1) GENERAL IMPRESSION
   What I am seeing?

2) PERSPECTIVE
   From where am I seeing it?
   Are there different planes?
   What is in each of them?

3) FEATURES
   a) Natural:
      – Relief forms?
      – Type of vegetation?
      – Are there rivers? What
        about rain? Is it more or
        less frequent?
      – What information gives
        me the colors?
   b) Human:
      – About settlement:
        ° Is there any?
          If yes, where is
          it placed? (coast,
          mountain, plain, near
          a river, etc.)
        ° If yes, what type is it?
          Rural? If so, is it
          concentrated or spread?
          Urban? If so, what is
          the form of the city?
          (Irregular, concentric,
          lineal, etc.)
          What type of functions
          does the city have?
          (Industrial, residential,
          commercial, tourism,
          etc.)
      – Communication routes
        Are there any? What
        type?
      – Economic activity
        Is there any? What type?
        (Agriculture, mining,
        fishery, industry, tourism,
        etc.)

4) INTERPRETATION
   What natural, human or both
   features contributed to the
   landscape looking the way it
   does?
   a) Natural
      – The type of soil?
      – Weather?
      – Erosion and
        sedimentation?
      – Earthquakes?
      – Constructing agents?
        (Volcanoes, coral, etc.)
   b) Human
      – What activities modify
        the landscape?
      – What effects do they
        have?

5) CLASSIFICATION
   – Is the landscape mostly
     natural – nature in a
     wild state?
     Why do I think that
     way?
   – Is the landscape mostly
     agrarian – are there
     farms and cultivation?
     Why do I think that
     way?
   – Is the landscape mostly
     industrial – are there
     factories?
     Why do I think that
     way?
   – Is the landscape mostly
     urban – are there human
     settlements?
     Why do I think that way?
   – In conclusion, what type
     of landscape is it? Why
     do I think that way?

   *Has this script helped me to do
   the landscape analysis?*

Figure 4.3 Script Designed to Help Students Learn How to Analyze a
Landscape
Source: Panadero, Alonso-Tapia, & Huertas, 2012.

and processes that an expert would apply to a task, particularly if you are a novice.

The challenge of composing a meaningful script in a complex learning domain should also not be understated. It is difficult to generate prompts that would simulate expert behavior but simultaneously adopt language and encourage processes accessible to a learner. Such an approach is unlikely to suit very young learners unless the script and the content being assessed are extremely simple.

Rubric-Guided Self-Assessment

One of the most promising and consistently endorsed forms of self-assessment is rubric-guided judgment (Andrade, 2010; Andrade & Valtcheva, 2009; Brown & Harris, 2013). A rubric provides criteria as well as hierarchically ordered levels, standards, or grades (e.g., basic, proficient, advanced) that describe different levels of quality. Holistic rubrics capture all important aspects or features of the work into an overall classification, while analytic rubrics specify various dimensions or components that are evaluated separately. Rubric-guided self-assessment, particularly when completed formatively during the learning, is considered to be particularly powerful as rubrics (a) make explicit the criteria describing quality work, allowing students to apply these to their own tasks, and (b) provide students with descriptors that can help them identify how to improve their performance (i.e., *In order to move from a C to a B, I need to make sure I . . .*).

Ideally, rubrics support self-assessment in all phases of a cycle of self-regulated learning. In the forethought or planning phase, the rubric can be introduced, helping students understand task objectives, set goals, and plan their actions. During the performance phase, students can use rubrics as part of metacognitive monitoring, allowing them to decide if their current work meets the standard of achievement they hope to accomplish and to identify what needs to be improved to achieve this goal. Finally, in the self-reflection phase, students can use the rubric to determine their final result; strengths and weaknesses identified through this process can then feed into goals for their next cycle of learning.

If rubrics are to be used for self-assessment, they should ideally be co-constructed with students (Newmann, Marks, & Gamoran, 1996). With judicious teacher prompting, a class-made scoring rubric can be developed, and co-constructing expectations in this way can have multiple benefits. First, rubrics that students co-construct are likely to be written in language they understand, making them far more user friendly for self-assessment purposes. Second, co-constructed rubrics allow students to provide input on what should be valued within the task. At times, students may have different perspectives about what is important than the teacher, and ignoring what students value may decrease their motivation to complete the task. Finally, the process of co-construction allows productive dialogue about the qualities of successful work, and multiple studies have found that such conversations lead to more accurate self-assessment and higher learning gains (Brown & Harris, 2013). If time or system constraints do not allow for co-construction, it is vital that teachers pay careful attention to the wording of rubrics used for self-assessment, making sure they are written in language students can easily understand and that time is taken to deconstruct them to ensure student understanding.

To illustrate the potential of this self-assessment technique, consider how the rubrics presented in Figures 4.4 and 4.5 were used to help students self-assess their work as part of the Arts Assessment for Learning project led by Maria Palma of the New York City Department of Education, Joanna Hefferen of ArtsConnection, and Heidi Andrade (for more details and access to additional rubrics and formative assessment tools, visit http://artsassessmentforlearning.org/). The rubric in Figure 4.4 was designed to help American fourth-grade students understand the characteristics of quality papier-mâché birds and to monitor their own progress toward creating these. What is particularly helpful is that the teacher has highlighted clear, observable distinctions between differing levels of performance (e.g., 4 = wire is very secure, 3 = wire needs some tape for more security, 2 = wire is wobbly and needs more tape, 1 = no wire).

RUBRIC: SCULPTURE: PAPIER MACHE BIRDS

	4	3	2	1
Building	Shape is firm	Shape is mostly firm	Shape is loose	What is this shape?
	All attachments are secure	One or two attachments need tape	All attachments need more tape	Missing some attachments
	Wire is very secure	Wire needs some tape for more security	Wire is wobbly and needs more tape	No wire
	Clearly balanced shape	Shape needs minor balancing	Lopsided shape - needs re-balancing	Shape needs to be completely rebalanced
Using papier-mâché	Evenly covers all the shape	Covers shape but needs evening out	Uneven coverage of shape, needs addition of papers	Little to no papier-mâché
	Smooth edges	A few open edges need to smoothed	Most edges need to be smoothed down	
	Tightly fits shape	Some loose places	Paper is too loose	
	Even wetness	Some dry spaces	Paper is too dry or too wet	
Painting	Colors touch or overlap	Some colors not touching or overlapping	Messy painting	No paint
	Evenly covers all paper	Some paper still visible	Mostly uncovered paper	
	Details clearly give feeling of texture	Details need to be further added for texture	Details need to be added	

Figure 4.4 Rubric for Fourth-Grade Visual Arts Project Around Making Paper-Mâché Birds
Source: Fremont, 2016, p. 1.

What I need to do next: Date: _____
_____

Artists I have studied: _____

What did I learn about sculpture today? _____

What problems will we have? Things to notice:

- Making the shape with newspaper. Is it firm?
- Handling and managing sticky tape. Are the attachments (wings, tail, head, beak) secure?
- Attaching the wire. Be careful with bending wire. Does is it stand? Is it balanced?
- Using the papier mache (methyl cellulose) and paper: MESSY Is the form completely covered with glue and paper? Did I help with clean up?

Painting

- Is the form completely covered with paint?
- Have I used a detail brush for small areas?
- Have I worked carefully?

Figure 4.4 (Continued)

Compare this approach to descriptors often used in rubrics like excellent, good, fair, and poor (which are based on the assumption that a student knows what *good* looks like and how this differs from *fair*).

The process of generating and using this rubric was also helpful for students. Although the teacher generated the final rubric, at the beginning of the unit, she shared examples of sculptures from previous years that represented varying levels of performance and had students identify "problems they might have" based on these examples and how to describe differences in the quality of performance. Below the rubric, the teacher also provided questions to help students monitor their process and included a section for students to use to reflect on what they

RUBRIC: RECORDER TECHNIQUE

	4	3	2	1
Fingering	My fingering is **perfect for each note**	My fingering is correct for **most** of the notes. I need help with . . .	I know **some** fingerings I get confused on many notes such as . . .	I do not know the fingering on the recorder. My next steps: 1. Make a fingering chart 2. Put notes together one at a time
Rhythm	The rhythm is **perfect** when I read it while fingering the notes.	**Most** of the rhythm patterns are perfect when I read them. OR The rhythms **are not** always perfect because I'm not sure of the fingering.	I know the rhythms one at a time, but not in a pattern. My next steps: 1. Practice slowly with a partner 2. Break-up sections when needed	I do not know the rhythms. My next steps: 1. Learn the rhythms 2. Put them together in 4 beat patterns
Sound/ Breath Support	The notes have a **pretty** sound. They do not squeak and I do not run out of breath	**Most** of the notes are pretty and smooth. There are a few squeaks. **Yellow** means I should work on the sound. This is where I run out of breath or the notes squeak.	**Some** parts sound pretty and smooth. **Yellow** means I should work on the sound. I am running out of breath a lot or the notes squeak.	The piece is hard to listen to. The notes sound pretty when I play them one at a time, but not when I put them together. My next step: 1. Practice slowly 2. Practice a few notes at a time

Figure 4.5 Rubric for Fourth- and Fifth-Grade Music Unit Around Learning to Play the Recorder
Source: Comba, 2016, p. 1.

| Phrasing | The phrasing sounds **pretty &** lyrical.

I am able to play phrase by phrase so that the notes do not sound ch-op-py and breath-y. | There are **some huff and puff** moments but most of the song was pretty.

Green means I need to work on making the phrasing smoother. | It's getting better.

There are phrases that still need **work**.

My next step:
1. Sing it with a partner

Green means I need to practice making notes sound smoooooth. | I know the notes, but it sounds like I am blowing out a birthday candle or huffing and puffing like the Big Bad Wolf!

My next step:
1. Practice 2 notes smoothly together and then add more so they sound smoooooooth |

Figure 4.5 (Continued)

had learned and what they needed to work on next. Such a tool clearly encourages students to consider the strengths and weaknesses of their own work and provides guidance as to what a more proficient performance might look like.

Another example is the rubric Comba (2016) devised to help her American grade 4 and 5 students self-assess their progress in learning to play a recorder (Figure 4.5). This rubric is particularly suited to self-assessment, using "I" and adopting language that learners would easily understand (e.g., 1 = "I know the notes, but it sounds like I am blowing out a birthday candle or huffing and puffing like the Big Bad Wolf!") rather than the more technical descriptions of standards found in syllabus documents. Another potentially useful feature here is the suggestions for next steps embedded within lower levels of the rubric. These provide learners who may realize they are currently at a low level of performance with clear ways to rectify this, a far more constructive approach than one in which students are asked just to identify the faults in their performance. When teaching her students to use the rubric, students were first walked through it, criterion by criterion, and then given the chance to practice using it while evaluating the teacher's performance (e.g., identifying in the music when the teacher played the wrong rhythm and then discussing how to score it on the rhythm criterion on the rubric). Because they had access to the rubric throughout the unit of work, they were able to use it when practicing at home and at school to remind themselves of the aspects of performance they needed to focus on (i.e., fingering, rhythm, sound/ breathing, phrasing), identify strengths and weaknesses in their current performance, and gain strategies to improve in specific areas of weakness.

Rubrics can be very useful for self-assessment, as they can help students rate their performance along a continuum according to appropriate criteria. Rubrics are thought to be particularly useful as they increase the transparency of expectations (which can reduce student anxiety; Andrade & Du, 2005), assist with the feedback process, and improve student self-efficacy and self-regulation (Panadero & Jonsson, 2013). Although self-assessment using rubrics often takes place during the performance and self-reflection phases, it should be introduced during the fore-thought phase because students need to know from the beginning the criteria and standards that describe work associated with various standards of quality.

Whether the rubric is externally sourced, teacher constructed, or co-constructed, the strength of rubric-based self-assessment compared to many of the other practices described previously is that it can be applied to a range of complex and challenging tasks (e.g., group projects, essays, presentations, performances). Rubrics can help students to make complex judgments about their work, moving beyond a dichotomous right/wrong approach to learning and assessment. Also, rubric-guided self-assessment can and should take place throughout the performance phase, providing students with a source of formative feedback as they identify where they currently are and what they still need to work on to reach their desired standard of performance.

The major challenge with this practice is reaching a shared understanding of criteria and standards, something that groups of teachers find difficult to do (Wyatt-Smith & Klenowski, 2012; Wyatt-Smith, Klenowski, & Gunn, 2010). Hence, considerable teacher time, either co-constructing or deconstructing criteria and standards with students, is needed to make sure students understand and can apply them accurately to their work. For example, a rubric that uses verbatim phrases from curriculum standards may be of little use to a primary school student, even though it may convey useful information to the teacher. Figures 4.4 and 4.5 show examples of rubrics that use language that even primary school students can appreciate and implement. For more advice on how to develop clear rubrics and share these with students, we highly recommend reading Chapter 3 of Andrade and Heritage's (2018) book, *Using Formative Assessment to Enhance Learning, Achievement, and Academic Self-Regulation.*

It is also important to realize that rubrics are time- and work-intensive. Considerable time is needed to first construct a clear and detailed rubric, with more required for explaining, exemplifying, and monitoring students' understanding of it. As each learning domain or content topic requires a different rubric, this process must be repeated for each new task to make sure students understand quality evaluation standards. Although this invest-ment of time is not a bad thing, when teaching is constrained by the need to cover curriculum content rapidly, then the processes of ensuring student understanding will be put at risk.

Although students may need a level of privacy, it is prob-ably important that such self-assessments, at least initially, are checked by the teacher to make sure that major misconceptions about what criteria mean can be resolved. Comba (2016) did this by getting her students to use the rubric found in Figure 4.5 to evaluate her own recorder performance before they attempted to self-assess. Their rubric-guided judgment of her performance was followed by a discussion during which they shared how they had applied criteria and standards, allowing major mis-conceptions to be identified and addressed before more private opportunities for self-assessment. However, if such an approach is not feasible, teachers can still check student self-assessment, focusing on whether the student has used the criteria realisti-cally rather than on how good the piece of work is (Brown & Harris, 2014). Once students become proficient in using rubrics to self-assess, it may be possible to use their evaluations as part of final course grades; however, due to the validity threats this can create, discussed more extensively in Chapter 3, formative uses are clearly safest.

Effectively Sequencing Self-Assessment Practices

We have argued previously about the importance of creating a self-assessment curriculum that clearly maps out how prac-tices can be sequenced in a developmentally appropriate way (Brown & Harris, 2014). Although such a curriculum is yet to be developed, we will now share our thoughts about how such sequencing might occur within K–12 education. All self-assessment practices can help students develop better metacognitive skills if used as a trigger for deeper reflection on their current abilities and what needs to occur for improvement in both self-assessment abilities and subject-area knowledge and skills to take place. Nonetheless, both theory and research consistently establish that rubrics, scripts, and more complex templates usually offer students more opportunities for learning and growth than self-marking and self-judgment of performance. Hence, it is highly advisable to develop student competencies so that they can engage effectively in more challenging versions of self-assessment. Realism in self-assessment is hard for students; although it is always challenging to identify your own level of performance, it is particularly hard when you (as a learner) know little about the domain. Particularly within complex domains, it is very hard to advance beyond the standing of a novice.

When starting self-assessment use for the first time, as a first step, we recommend getting students to self-assess in relation to relatively objective aspects of the curriculum (e.g., spelling, grammar, mathematical computation, recall of facts). For example, students may begin with simple estimates of performance (e.g., *How many spelling words will I get right this week?*) or self-marking (e.g., marking the spelling quiz against an answer key). Simple rubrics that attend to primarily objective aspects of performance (e.g., number of spelling errors) may also be effective. Such opportunities will help learners develop the habit of checking their own work and identifying their own mistakes. It will also allow them start to see themselves as assessment capable, an important mindset to develop before they embark on more cognitively challenging self-assessment activities. Given the objective nature of these aspects of the curriculum, it will also help students develop accuracy in self-assessment and see this as something to be valued.

The next step involves getting students to add a dimension of narrative feedback in which they identify strengths, weaknesses, and next learning steps from their own work. Going back to the spelling test example, can the student identify any connections between the words he or she got right or wrong (e.g., *I seem to be having trouble spelling words that have a silent vowel*) or fundamental problems with his or her approach to the task (e.g., *I have not spent enough time this week learning my words* or *The strategies I am using to help me remember my words are not working*)? Students can then be taught to formulate next learning steps. For example, *I need to review the spelling rules around words that have a silent vowel* or *Perhaps I should study differently this week; I could make myself flash cards.*

Once students are comfortable doing this, the next step is to get them to try to self-assess work where criteria and standards are more abstract or implicit (e.g., writing, art, historical argument). To self-assess accurately in such domains, students need to engage in discussions about the criteria and standards as related to quality work and to internalize such standards. Initially, it may be with simple checklists or templates about structures or features that are relatively easy to pick out (e.g., *Does each of my paragraphs have a topic sentence?*). However, the goal is to move students along to the point where they can use scripts or rubrics to evaluate complex performances. Co-constructing rubrics can help students better understand what standards mean and how to apply them to their work (Andrade & Heritage, 2018). Because teachers often disagree about how criteria and standards should be interpreted, this is not an easy task. It seems important to give credit to self-assessors who make a credible argument, using evidence from their own work, to make a case for their self-assessment.

There are some important caveats to this recommended progression. First, the sequence has been designed on principles derived from the literature we have discussed so far. We have no concrete research evidence as yet that these recommendations constitute the most effective way to teach students to self-assess. To our knowledge, there has not been any longitudinal work done to establish the long-term effectiveness of this or any other suggested self-assessment progression. Nonetheless, this sequence makes sense to us, and we look forward to reports as to the validity of this recommendation.

Second, the sequence assumes teachers are treating self-assessment as a skill to be learned rather than as just a mechanism for curriculum content learning. This means that as teachers enact more complex and challenging self-assessment practices with students, they need to clearly explain to them why they are participating in this particular form of assessment rather than just using it as a vehicle for content learning. Students need to know how to recognize when they are coming to appropriate judgments (and when they are not) and what to do with the self-assessment feedback they are providing to themselves.

Furthermore, like any learned skill, teachers must monitor student development and only move them on to more challenging forms as they demonstrate competence or as the learning material requires it. This does not mean that teachers should not use rubrics or scripts with students until they are competent self-assessors. It just means they need to carefully consider the complexity of the rubric or script and to ensure that initial student use of such a tool focuses on a limited number of features, with a greater focus on more objective rather than on more abstract or implicit features. Likewise, due to student prior knowledge and experience, teachers may not need to start at the beginning of this progression. Upper primary, secondary, and tertiary students may have previous understanding of or experience with self-assessment (even if it was informal or self-directed) that may allow them to engage immediately with such approaches as rubric-guided self-assessment or scripts.

The key is that you as a teacher must evaluate where your students are at and move them forward accordingly. It is important to remember that there are two goals here: (1) improvement in challenging skills, knowledge, and abilities and (2) the ability to realistically self-assess one's own work, including identification of weaknesses and strengths. Attainment of the first goal is greatly enhanced by conscious attention to the second.

The Impact of Technology on Self-Assessment Practices

As a final note, when planning self-assessment implementation, consider the impact technology may have on these practices now and into the future. As more and more assessment is being conducted via digital platforms (Katz & Gorin, 2016), an important area of inquiry involves investigating how this mode can be best harnessed for self-assessment purposes. At this point, to our knowledge, use of technology doesn't appear to have fundamentally changed the kind of self-assessment tasks school students are being asked to do (e.g., using rating scales, doing Traffic Lights–type tasks, using clickers). In light of this, digital self-assessment practices were not treated as a separate category per se within this chapter.

However, it is clear that using technology does have the potential to help make self-assessment more private and/or anonymous (e.g., students could share the Traffic Lights self-assessment directly with the teacher or anonymously via clickers or polling software without peers being aware of their assessment). Although there are studies that examine self-assessment practices conducted via technology (e.g., Sung, Chang, Chang, & Yu, 2010), we are unaware of any studies that explicitly investigate if the process of conducting self-assessment via a computer or electronic device changes the way students engage with the self-assessment task (e.g., Does it increase or decrease student motivation or make it harder or easier for students to evaluate their work in the manner expected?). It is worth noting that e-portfolios often require reflective comments, but the assessment of these comments is largely left to the human reading the self-assessment (San Jose, 2017).

In the future, we can expect that digital self-assessment may be a very promising space as it may improve privacy while still allowing students to receive feedback (e.g., feedback on the accuracy of a student's self-assessment may come from a computer source or an anonymous peer), but there is much still that needs to be explored. Digitizing self-assessment may also introduce new concerns; for instance, teachers will need to verify that digital self-assessment systems provide adequate privacy and data security (Tierney & Koch, 2016). As teachers begin to move more self-assessment into digital formats, we encourage them to continue to think mindfully about the key issues we have discussed in this and the previous chapter. Regardless of whether students are using a computer interface or a pen and piece of paper to engage in self-assessment, they still need to have access to clear criteria to guide self-assessments of their work (which have been co-constructed or deconstructed to ensure their understanding) and to be able to conduct self-assessments in a psychologically safe space where they are supported to identify strengths and weaknesses without unnecessary threats to ego or self-esteem.

Summary

This chapter has described some of the most common forms of self-assessment used in schools, highlighting strengths and weaknesses associated with each. Practices explored included the following:

- Estimating future performance
- Simple self-ratings
- Self-marking
- Self-assessment templates
- Self-assessment scripts
- Rubric-guided self-assessment

It is appropriate to use some of the simpler techniques (i.e., estimating future performance, simple self-ratings, self-marking), particularly with younger students, to help them adjust to the idea of assessing their own work and to gain a clearer picture of the accuracy of their own assessments. However, it is vital that they do eventually learn to self-assess in ways that require them to justify their judgments and to analyze their work during and after more complex and nonobjective tasks.

What we hope has become apparent in this chapter is that although practices enabling complex judgments (e.g., rubric-based self-assessment, use of scripts) are able to work with a wider range of curriculum objectives and help students engage in more complex metacognitive processes, as Dinsmore and Wilson (2016) note, there are no practices that automatically generate self-regulation and deeper level learning. How much students will gain from the self-assessment process is highly contingent on how it is implemented. For example, students may learn quite a lot and get opportunities to self-regulate from a simple self-marking activity if part of the task is to go back and look carefully at how their responses differ from the correct answers, fix their mistakes, and then complete some similar activities to reinforce the learned skill before attempting the task again. Conversely, if students are asked just to make a judgment using a simple rubric but are not asked to explain or justify their evaluations or are not expected to do anything to develop any weaknesses identified, little is likely to be gained from the exercise. Additionally, self-assessment is unlikely to be helpful to students unless they clearly understand the criteria and standards they are using to make their judgments.

Teachers need to slowly build and develop student self-assessment capabilities so that as students progress through school, they are able to make more complex judgments about their work, as these will help them to set appropriate goals and to accurately monitor their progress toward reaching them. We recommend starting with self-assessment activities that are used to evaluate tasks with fairly objective responses (e.g., mathematics tasks, spelling/grammar activities, multiple-choice quizzes) because doing this will allow students to check their self-evaluations without needing substantial input from teachers or peers. Once students understand the purpose of self-assessment and have had a little bit of practice doing this, it is important that teachers support students to engage in more complex forms of self-assessment (e.g., using a rubric to evaluate an essay, examining problem-solving processes using a script). Following this progression will help develop students' curriculum knowledge and their self-assessment skills. Although this chapter has focused on the strengths and weaknesses of varying self-assessment techniques and how to potentially sequence them, the final chapter of this book explores how to implement self-assessment effectively within individual classrooms as well as across groups (e.g., year levels, departments) and schools.

References

Andrade, H. (2010). Students as the definitive source of formative assessment: Academic self-assessment and the self-regulation of learning. In H. L. Andrade & G. J. Cizek (Eds.), *Handbook of formative assessment* (pp. 90–105). New York, NY: Routledge.

Andrade, H. (in press). Feedback in the Context of Self-assessment. In A. Lipnevich & J. K. Smith (Eds.), *The Cambridge Handbook of Instructional Feedback*. Cambridge, UK: Cambridge University Press.

Andrade, H., & Du, Y. (2005). Student perspectives on rubric-referenced assessment. *Practical Assessment, Research, and Evaluation, 10(3)*, 1–11.

Andrade, H., & Heritage, M. (2018). *Using formative assessment to enhance learning, achievement, and academic self-regulation.* New York, NY: Routledge.

Andrade, H., & Valtcheva, A. (2009). Promoting learning and achievement through self-assessment. *Theory into Practice, 28*(1), 12–19.

Assessment for Learning Resources. (2011). *Two stars and a wish.* Retrieved from www.tes.com/teaching-resource/assessment-for-learning-resources-6110419

Baars, M., Vink, S., van Gog, T., de Bruin, A., & Paas, F. (2014). Effects of training self-assessment and using assessment standards on retrospective and prospective monitoring of problem solving. *Learning & Instruction, 33*, 92–107. doi:10.1016/j.learninstruc.2014.04.004

Black, P., Harrison, C., Lee, C., Marshall, B., & Wiliam, D. (2003). *Assessment for learning: Putting it into practice.* Maidenhead, England: Open University Press.

Brookhart, S. M. (2016). Building assessments that work in the classroom. In G. T. L. Brown & L. R. Harris (Eds.), *Handbook of human and social conditions in assessment* (pp. 351–365). New York, NY: Routledge.

Brown, G. T. L. (2018). *Assessment of student achievement.* New York, NY: Routledge.

Brown, G. T. L., & Harris, L. R. (2013). Student self-assessment. In J. H. McMillan (Ed.), *Sage handbook of research on classroom assessment* (pp. 367–393). Thousand Oaks, CA: Sage.

Brown, G. T. L., & Harris, L. R. (2014). The future of self-assessment in classroom practice: Reframing self-assessment as a core competency. *Frontline Learning Research, 3*, 22–30. doi:10.14786/flr.v2i1.24

Brown, G. T. L., Peterson, E. R., & Irving, S. E. (2009). Beliefs that make a difference: Adaptive and maladaptive self-regulation in students' conceptions of assessment. In D. M. McInerney, G. T. L. Brown, & G. A. D. Liem (Eds.), *Student perspectives on assessment: What students can tell us about assessment for learning* (pp. 159–186). Charlotte, NC: Information Age.

Brown, G. T. L., Peterson, E. R., & Yao, E. (2016). Student conceptions of feedback: Impact on self-regulation, self-efficacy, and academic achievement. *British Journal of Educational Psychology, 86*(4), 606–629. doi:10.1111/bjep.12126

Clarke, S. (2001). *Unlocking formative assessment: Practical strategies for enhancing pupil's learning in the primary classroom.* London, England: Hodder Education.

Clarke, S. (2005). *Formative assessment in the secondary classroom.* London, England: Hodder Murray.

Clarke, S., Timperley, H. S., & Hattie, J. A. (2003). *Unlocking formative assessment: Practical strategies for enhancing students' learning in the primary and intermediate classroom.* Auckland, New Zealand: Hodder Moa Beckett.

Comba, M. (2016). *Recorder technique: Peer and self-assessment.* Retrieved from http://artsassessmentforlearning.org/project/recorder-technique/

Covington, M. V., & Teel, K. M. (1996). *Overcoming student failure: Changing motives and incentives for learning.* Washington, DC: American Psychological Association.

Cowie, B. (2009). My teacher and my friends help me learn: Student perspectives and experiences of classroom assessment. In D. M. McInerney, G. T. L. Brown, & G. A. D. Liem (Eds.), *Student perspectives on assessment: What students can tell us about assessment for learning* (pp. 85–105). Charlotte, NC: Information Age.

Dinsmore, D. L., & Wilson, H. E. (2016). Student participation in assessment: Does it influence self-regulation. In G. T. L. Brown & L. R. Harris (Eds.), *Handbook of human and social conditions in assessment* (pp. 145–168). New York, NY: Routledge.

Dunning, D., Heath, C., & Suls, J. M. (2004). Flawed self-assessment: Implications for health, education, and the workplace. *Psychological Science in the Public Interest, 5*(3), 69–106.

Fletcher, A. K. (2016). Exceeding expectations: Scaffolding agentic engagement through assessment as learning. *Educational Research, 58*(4), 400–419. doi:10.1080/00131881.2016.1235909

Fletcher, A. K. (2017). Help seeking: Agentic learners initiating feedback. *Educational Review,* Advanced online publication. doi: 10.1080/00131911.2017.1340871

Fremont, A. (2016). *Papier mache sculpture: Self and peer assessment.* Retrieved from http://artsassessmentforlearning.org/project/papier-mache-sculpture/

Harris, L. R., & Brown, G. T. L. (2013). Opportunities and obstacles to consider when using peer- and self-assessment to improve student learning: Case studies into teachers' implementation. *Teaching and Teacher Education, 36,* 101–111. doi:10.1016/j.tate.2013.07.008

Harris, L. R., Brown, G. T. L., & Dargusch, J. (2018). Not playing the game: Student assessment resistance as a form of agency. *Australian Educational Researcher, 45*(1), 125–140. doi:10.1007/s13384-018-0264-0

Harris, L. R., Brown, G. T. L., & Harnett, J. A. (2015). Analysis of New Zealand primary and secondary student peer- and self-assessment comments: Applying Hattie and Timperley's feedback model.

Assessment in Education: Principles, Policy & Practice, 22(2), 265–281. doi:10.1080/0969594x.2014.976541

Hattie, J. (2009). *Visible learning: A synthesis of meta-analyses in education.* London, England: Routledge.

Katz, I. R., & Gorin, J. S. (2016). Computerising assessment: Impacts on education stakeholders. In G. T. L. Brown & L. R. Harris (Eds.), *Handbook of human and social conditions in assessment* (pp. 472–489). New York, NY: Routledge.

Leahy, S., Lyon, C., Thompson, M., & Wiliam, D. (2005). Classroom assessment: Minute by minute, day by day. *Educational Leadership, 63*(3), 19–24.

Meyer, L. H., McClure, J., Walkey, F., Weir, K. F., & McKenzie, L. (2009). Secondary student motivation orientations and standards-based achievement outcomes. *British Journal of Educational Psychology, 79*(2), 273–293. doi:10.1348/000709908X354591

Murdock, T. B., Stephens, J. M., & Groteweil, M. M. (2016). Student dishonesty in the face of assessment: Who, why, and what we can do about it. In G. T. L. Brown & L. R. Harris (Eds.), *Handbook of human and social conditions in assessment* (pp. 186–203). New York, NY: Routledge.

Nelson, T. O., & Narens, L. (1990). Metamemory: A theoretical framework and new findings. *The Psychology of Learning and Motivation, 26*, 125–141.

Newmann, F. M., Marks, H. M., & Gamoran, A. (1996). Authentic pedagogy and student performance. *American Journal of Education, 104*(4), 280–312. doi:10.1086/444136

Panadero, E., Alonso-Tapia, J., & Huertas, J. A. (2012). Rubrics and self-assessment scripts effects on self-regulation, learning and self-efficacy in secondary education. *Learning and Individual Differences, 22*(6), 806–813. doi:10.1016/j.lindif.2012.04.007

Panadero, E., & Jonsson, A. (2013). The use of scoring rubrics for formative assessment purposes revisited: A review. *Educational Research Review, 9*, 129–144. doi:10.1016/j.edurev.2013.01.002

Panadero, E., Jonsson, A., & Strijbos, J.-W. (2016). Scaffolding self-regulated learning through self-assessment and peer assessment: Guidelines for classroom implementation. In D. Laveault & L. Allal (Eds.), *Assessment for learning: Meeting the challenge of implementation* (pp. 311–326). Cham, Switzerland: Springer International.

Powel, W. D., & Gray, R. (1995). Improving performance predictions by collaboration with peers and rewarding accuracy. *Child Study Journal, 25*(2), 141–154.

Rotsaert, T., Panadero, E., Schellens, T., & Raes, A. (2017). "Now you know what you're doing right and wrong!" Peer feedback quality in synchronous peer assessment in secondary education. *European Journal of Psychology of Education*, Advanced online publication. doi:10.1007/s10212-017-0329-x

Sadler, P. M., & Good, E. (2006). The impact of self- and peer-grading on student learning. *Educational Assessment*, *11*(1), 1–31.

San Jose, D. L. (2017). Evaluating, comparing, and best practice in electronic portfolio system use. *Journal of Educational Technology Systems*, *45*(4), 476–498. doi:10.1177/0047239516672049

Sung, Y.-T., Chang, K.-E., Chang, T.-H., & Yu, W.-C. (2010). How many heads are better than one? The reliability and validity of teenagers' self- and peer assessments. *Journal of Adolescence*, *33*(1), 135–145. doi:10.1016/j.adolescence.2009.04.004

Sweller, J. (2006). The worked example effect and human cognition. *Learning & Instruction*, *16*(2), 165–169.

Tierney, R. D., & Koch, M. J. (2016). Privacy in classroom assessment. In G. T. L. Brown & L. R. Harris (Eds.), *Handbook of human and social conditions in assessment* (pp. 267–283). New York, NY: Routledge.

Webb, M., & Jones, J. (2009). Exploring tensions in developing assessment for learning. *Assessment in Education: Principles, Policy & Practice*, *16*(2), 165–184. doi:10.1080/09695940903075925

Wyatt-Smith, C., & Klenowski, V. (2012). Explicit, latent and meta-criteria: Types of criteria at play in professional judgment practice. *Assessment in Education: Principles, Policy & Practice*, *20*(1), 35–52. doi:10.1080/0969594x.2012.725030

Wyatt-Smith, C., Klenowski, V., & Gunn, S. (2010). The centrality of teachers' judgment practice in assessment: A study of standards in moderation. *Assessment in Education: Principles, Policy & Practice*, *17*(1), 59–75. doi:10.1080/09695940903565610

Yan, Z., & Brown, G. T. L. (2017). A cyclical self-assessment process: Towards a model of how students engage in self-assessment. *Assessment & Evaluation in Higher Education*, *42*(8), 1247–1262. doi:10.1080/02602938.2016.126009

5

Implementing Self-Assessment in Classrooms and Schools

By this point in the book, we hope you are convinced that self-assessment is a useful tool and that you have started to formulate plans around how you can incorporate it into your classroom and/or school. However, we have also pointed out that implementation is far from straightforward; self-assessment is a complex practice. Although all classroom assessment practices have many variables to keep in mind (e.g., purpose, developmental appropriateness, alignment with curriculum and what was taught, timing), self-assessment has an additional layer of complexity. To successfully self-assess, students must be supported to overcome instincts toward ego protection, enabling them to identify potential misunderstandings and shortcomings in their work. It is also a practice that will only be effective if students have a clear understanding of learning goals and what quality work looks like. Simultaneously, classroom self-assessment takes place in a complex psychosocial space where concerns about disclosure to peers and the teacher can thwart its intentions. Hence, in order to implement self-assessment in ways that will maximize its benefits for learning, you need to carefully plan student self-assessment opportunities, monitor practices while they are ongoing to identify and mediate potential challenges, and reflectively determine students' next learning steps both around curriculum targets and self-regulation competencies.

This chapter is designed to help guide you as you work to implement self-assessment, both within your own teaching space and as you collaborate with others across your school or department. Although it may be natural to evaluate yourself and your actions, self-assessment practices that will actually lead to improved self-regulation and learning are learned behaviors. They are realistic, systematic, and based on curriculum standards and expectations rather than on an individual's personal opinions about what is important or what will best protect his or her ego.

We have found it helpful if teachers think of implementing self-assessment as part of their own cyclical process of self-regulated learning. Zimmerman's (2008) model encourages learners to engage in forethought, performance, and self-reflective phases; these are also highly beneficial for the classroom teacher or school leader to follow if he or she is serious about quality self-assessment implementation. In our experience, facilitating quality student self-assessment begins with careful planning (the forethought phase). Next, actively monitor implementation, making adjustments when necessary (the performance phase). Finally, gather data about how it went (the self-reflection phase), and reflect on these data as information that will feed into the planning of the next self-assessment activity. It is only through this kind of careful and systematic implementation that self-assessment's goals will be achieved.

Forethought Phase

Like most quality teaching and learning practices, self-assessment must start with careful planning. Teachers must consider many things, including the following:

- The influence of school and district policy
- Their rationale for using self-assessment

- Students' beliefs about and previous experiences with self-assessment
- What self-assessment tasks to select and when to use them

Identifying School and District Policies Around Self-Assessment

One of the first considerations needs to center around external expectations within your school and/or district. Although self-assessment has never (to our knowledge) been legally restricted or banned within an educational jurisdiction (unlike peer grading, which was made illegal in six states in America until the Supreme Court overturned the ruling; Sadler & Good, 2006), it is important to first establish your school's and district's policies around self-assessment and how such data can be collected and used. For example:

- What kinds of self-assessment practices are currently in use and/or encouraged within your school or schooling system?
- How much flexibility and pedagogical freedom are teachers within your system allowed?
- Will the self-assessment practices you are considering align well with your school's and district's expectations?
- Is self-assessment required at your school?
- Can or must self-assessment be included when formulating a course grade?

One aspect that is particularly important to investigate is how self-assessment relates to grades. We and many others advise that it is best to keep self-assessment formative rather than evaluative. Excluding self-assessment from grading removes a major incentive for student dishonesty or manipulation of self-assessment (Andrade, 2010; Andrade & Brown, 2016; Harris & Brown, 2013). Why would students want to accurately identify their own mistakes if they know this will mean they will receive a lower grade? However, within some jurisdictions, there is considerable pressure to allocate points or grades to all classroom activities. If this is the case, how would you "grade" the self-assessment (e.g., points for participation, accuracy, depth of justification)? In contexts where teachers are required to assign points or scores for self-assessment, the most logical compromise would be to award a small proportion of the total grade for the task (e.g., 5%) for active and engaged participation in the self-assessment process. This would recognize the effort involved but would not provide incentive for students to inflate their self-assessment results in hopes of attaining a better grade.

It is also important to consider parent viewpoints because their support or opposition can strongly influence particular school-level practices. Parents use assessment data to understand how their children are progressing toward standards and expectations, and they may be uncomfortable about receiving evaluations from anyone but the teacher due to concerns about clarity and accuracy (Harris & Brown, 2016; Ross, 2006). As one student in Peterson and Irving's (2008) study noted, "[Parents] *care more about what my teacher would have to say about me, not what I would have to say about me*" (p. 246). Clearly, if parents do not value self-assessment, their opinions can undermine their children's support of such practices. If you are one of the first teachers to use self-assessment at your school, or you are working with children who are in their first year or two at your school, it would seem advisable to communicate with parents about your use of self-assessment within the classroom, explaining what their children are expected to gain from the practice.

Determining Why Self-Assessment Is Being Used

Before choosing strategies, it is vital that you think carefully about what you want to accomplish via self-assessment. Sadler and Good (2006) identify four possible reasons for self-assessment, specifically in relation to the practice of self-marking, although equally applicable to other self-assessment practices as well: logistical, pedagogical, metacognitive, and affective. These differing purposes will guide you in selecting various practices.

Logistical Reasons

Logistical reasons primarily relate to how student self-assessment may allow students to receive feedback more quickly and reduce the teacher's marking workload. These purposes will usually align best with self-marking activities. For example, if students self-mark an assessment, they get almost instantaneous feedback; if the teacher grades it, it may be days before the work is returned to the students given that most teachers' marking takes place outside of school hours. Grading may also take teacher time away from other valuable activities, such as planning, interacting with students, or reflecting on the effectiveness of current teaching.

Although teachers can get students to self-assess work in a range of ways (e.g., using rubrics, answer keys), it is important for teachers to realize that if logistics are the main purpose, it may be best to use it in conjunction with tasks that have primarily objective responses. More complex forms of self-assessment (e.g., using a rubric to grade a written assignment, guided self-assessment via a complex template) will require significant scaffolding. Teachers will also likely need to moderate the process and results to make sure students have understood the criteria and standards in the way intended and have applied them accurately. Hence, these kinds of self-assessment are not likely to save much, if any, teacher time.

Pedagogical Reasons

Teachers may choose to use self-assessment for pedagogical reasons if their main purpose is to help students more deeply learn their subject's content and skills. As noted by McMillan (2018), mistakes are a vital part of the learning process. Self-assessment may be designed to help students identify and engage with their mistakes. When a teacher marks a task, it is easy for students to focus on the grade or narrative comments without looking carefully through the whole piece of work to identify its strengths and weaknesses. Students' knowledge of the subject matter they are trying to learn is likely to increase if they take the time to identify and understand accurately the strengths and weaknesses within their work. Applications of self-assessment stemming from this purpose are likely to be highly focused on the content being self-assessed and designed to support students in learning the harder aspects of a content domain. Hence, the teacher has to support such goals by providing extra time for revision, engaging in robust discussions around quality, and giving feedback.

Metacognitive Reasons

Self-assessment might also be conducted to try to improve metacognitive processes (e.g., ability to self-evaluate, generate feedback), teaching students to self-regulate their learning. Learning how to judge work according to criteria and standards is an important academic skill in its own right and one that is highly valuable not only at school but also within the workplace. Furthermore, this process helps students develop higher order thinking skills. This purpose will lead to implementation that directs learners' attention to improving their skills in relation to the process of self-assessment itself. The content being learned is more of a vehicle to develop a lifelong learning competency. Learning to identify and act on their weaknesses will help prepare students for future life and workplace situations. Hence, this approach can be used in all content domains that have abstract and sometimes implicit standards of quality. Nonetheless, this is a time-consuming approach for both teachers and students and may engender some resistance from those expecting students to focus on learning content knowledge.

Affective Reasons

Finally, there may be affective motives for engaging students in self-assessment. Teachers may choose to use self-assessment as a way to help students develop agency, take control of their learning, and increase self-efficacy (Panadero, Jonsson, & Botella, 2017). It can also help students develop more positive mind-sets toward tests and evaluations in general by helping them better understand how such results are generated.

Receiving grades or marks from a teacher that students don't understand can be demoralizing and lead to lower motivation (*Why did I only get a C?*) or can lead to a dislike of particular assessment genres (*I don't like tests because they just judge me and don't help me learn*). Participation in self-assessment can potentially demystify the evaluation process and help students feel more empowered because they have a clearer idea of what they need to do in order to improve. If students evaluate themselves, the feedback they produce will be in language they understand, making it easier to use.

If affective reasons, such as increasing motivation and confidence, are the primary motivators for self-assessment, it may be possible to allow students to provide substantial input around the criteria used for assessment, even if these criteria are not entirely aligned with curriculum expectations (e.g., students may choose to include effort as a criterion). Allowing, supporting, and encouraging students to assess their work using their own standards may help learners to develop autonomy and authority over their work. Additionally, in these instances, self-assessment accuracy may be less important, at least initially, given that the focus is on developing positive attitudes toward self-assessment and increasing their self-efficacy as assessors. Nonetheless, we would urge teachers and students to work together to develop realistic evaluations of work quality, underpinned by the belief that all students can improve and that teachers can support this improvement.

Clearly, these four purposes are not mutually exclusive, and self-assessment practices can be implemented for multiple reasons. However, teachers must think carefully about the primary reason for using self-assessment in each instance. Is it mostly to save time and speed up the feedback process? Is it to assist students to master the subject content they are trying to learn? Is it to help students learn how to self-regulate? Or is it to help motivate and empower students? Remember that over a period of time, you can use self-assessment for any combination of these purposes, but it is worthwhile to have clear in your mind what the main purpose or purposes are for each implementation so that the enacted practices align with these goals.

Considering Students' Previous Experiences of and Beliefs About Self-Assessment

As we have suggested previously, it is important that students are given the chance to learn how to self-assess; competency cannot be assumed. Like any skill, it is imperative that students start with concrete and simple versions of self-assessment (e.g., marking a spelling quiz using an answer key, using a rubric that focuses on a limited number of fairly objective qualities within the work) before moving on to more complex and abstract types (e.g., using a rubric to judge the creativity of an idea within a piece of writing, evaluating the depth of understanding of complex concepts within a science report). Remember that younger students may not be cognitively ready to participate in complex forms of self-assessment (e.g., where they have to bring together evaluations of multiple criteria to form a holistic judgment).

Research shows that younger and academically weaker students tend to be overly optimistic when judging their own work (Brown & Harris, 2013), so such students may require more initial opportunities for feedback on the accuracy of their self-assessment claims. Nonetheless, some students may find the reality of their results difficult to accept at any age or stage. This is a powerful reason to help students be aware of the challenge that growth places on ego.

Likewise, it is well documented that although many students approach self-assessment positively, there are several negative beliefs they may hold that can undermine their self-assessments. Studies have repeatedly found that students are likely to doubt their own competence as assessors, especially initially (Brown & Harris, 2013). As one Canadian student in Ross, Rolheiser, and Hogaboam-Gray's (1998) study explained,

> Well, we really don't know how to mark ourselves. Since it's from our point of view, we may think it's good . . . But with the teacher marking, it's fair, they're trained to mark and they can find what's wrong.

(p. 471)

Some students simply deny that self-assessment is part of their role as learners or may fear it will mean less access to helpful teacher feedback (Harris & Brown, 2013). Students may be stuck in a paradigm where they believe that only teacher opinions about their work matter (Peterson & Irving, 2008), or they may devalue it because "*usually it doesn't count* [for grades or points], *so there is no point in doing it*" (Ross et al., 1998, p. 473). Likewise, students may be concerned that it allows their classmates to cheat (Harris & Brown, 2013). As one student in Ross et al.'s (1998) Canadian study said, "*People could take advantage of it and just mark all perfect when it's really not to their best ability*" (p. 471).

Our research has taught us that student (and teacher) mindsets really matter, so it is important to consider how you will convince students that self-assessment is a valuable skill to develop and work to alleviate any fears or concerns they may have about their participation. Although young students may not need to know and understand theoretical models of self-regulated learning, they can be taught basic principles of self-regulation as part of meta-talk about the things 'good learners do.' Even young learners can be encouraged to think about a cyclical process of self-regulation if such terms as those we shared in Chapter 2 (i.e., appraising and planning, doing and monitoring, evaluating and reflecting) are translated into language they can understand. The more language around self-regulation becomes part of how teachers and students talk about learning within the classroom, the greater the chance that self-regulation will be attained.

Likewise, now that you are aware of many of the concerns students may have about self-assessment (e.g., worries about their own accuracy and competence, concerns about disclosing self-evaluations to teachers and peers, problems with understanding why and how to self-assess), you can take active steps to address these before learners engage in the process. You can help dispel any concerns through whole-class discussions about potential problems and how they will be addressed. If students may not be confident enough to publically raise issues, an alternative approach might be to establish an anonymous class suggestions box that students could use to voice problems or concerns that you could then address with the group.

If you are unsure of how your students feel about self-assessment, it may be worthwhile to simply ask them about it. Two interesting methods of collecting student perceptions of assessment techniques could be applied here: (1) a standardized self-report inventory about assessment (Brown, 2011) or (2) a free-response drawing exercise in which students draw their take on assessment (Harris, Harnett, & Brown, 2009). These techniques, as well as direct discussion (via more formal focus groups or interviews or informal class discussions), can inform you as to what steps you may need to take in order to get students to value self-assessment practices in your classroom.

Selecting an Appropriate Self-Assessment Technique and When It Will Occur

Once teachers have considered policy expectations, determined why they want to use self-assessment, and have considered their students' previous experiences with and thoughts about self-assessment, the next step is to determine the specific qualities you want students to attend to within their work. For example, in a writing task, you could get them to focus on self-assessing from among myriad important aspects within composition (e.g., spelling, grammar, text structure, voice, ideas, vocabulary). Likewise, within a science experiment, there are different aspects that warrant attention (e.g., design, selection of materials and instruments, procedures, description of results, inferences or conclusions, clarity of writing or structure).

We suggest that you plan to keep self-assessment closely aligned with the specific learning intention or focus of the lesson and/or unit. If you have been doing a unit of work around descriptive language, get students to self-assess for use of description only rather than asking them to evaluate the overall quality of their text or simultaneously check for other features, such as grammar and mechanics. In this way, students will be self-assessing the learning intentions or goals in focus rather than their overall skill or competence within the domain.

Once you know specifically what you want students to self-assess within their own work, the next step is to select an appropriate technique to structure that self-assessment. Consider students' previous experience with self-assessments, their developmental levels, and their policy expectations. At the end of Chapter 4, we recommended how you might sequence self-assessment techniques. These suggestions focused on providing students with scaffolding toward making more complex judgments and justifications. It is important to consider this developmental progression and to gauge what might be an appropriate starting point for your students. Remember that even if you select a particular technique (e.g., rubric-guided self-assessment), it is possible to implement this in ways that are simple or complex. For example, there is a big difference between asking students to use a rubric or rating scale that focuses on concrete features (e.g., 1 = no spelling errors, 2 = one to three spelling errors, 3 = four or more spelling errors) and expecting them to apply narrative criteria to a more subjective aspect of the work (e.g., evaluate the creativity of ideas within a short story they have written).

Timing is another key feature to address within the planning phase. While we recommend that students are asked to self-assess throughout the learning cycle, you still need to identify specific points in time for this to occur. For example, it may be useful to have students self-assess the quality of their planning, their work in progress, and their work at the end.

Different techniques may be used in various parts of the cycle. For example, you might draw on a template, such as the one Fletcher (2016) designed (included in Chapter 4), that allows students to set goals at the beginning of their tasks and then monitor their progress repeatedly throughout the process of learning. You might choose to start a unit by deconstructing or co-constructing a rubric and then allowing students to check their progress against it at key points (e.g., before they share a first draft with a peer for peer review, when they think they are almost ready to submit a final version of the task). You might combine techniques, or if your focus is on developing realism, you may draw primarily on self-marking at the end of an activity or on a prospective self-judgment of performance at the beginning.

The point is that you need to know from the outset when and how self-assessment will fit into your unit of work. This will help you make sure that you have included time following self-assessment activities where students can deliberately use the feedback from their self-assessments to make improvements to their work or to seek help for issues they do not know how to address.

Finally, as mentioned when we were discussing the policy context, you must consider carefully what part, if any, self-assessment results will have in relation to students' grades. This decision may be out of your hands given school or district expectations. If so, you need to think carefully about how you can best work within system guidelines to protect the integrity and learning benefits of the self-assessment techniques you have selected. Although keeping self-assessment ungraded and formative will minimize some of the concerns identified in Chapter 3 (e.g., students purposely falsifying self-assessment results to obtain a better grade), many students have been trained to invest effort only in things that 'count' toward their results. Clearly, we do not want to deny students the right to be strategic with their time, but ungraded self-reflection does have learning benefits, and teachers need to help students see the value in such processes. Hence, decisions around what techniques to use and when should be made only after carefully considering your individual students.

Performance Phase

Although the majority of the work underpinning quality self-assessment practices within the classroom occurs in the forethought or planning phase, it is vital that teachers actively monitor student self-assessment activities during the performance or implementation phase. By monitoring and reflecting on what students report is happening in the moment for themselves, you are able to make adjustments in response to that feedback. For this to happen, however, you need to actively manage psychosocial variables (e.g., classroom relationships) in order to help students feel that the classroom is a safe place where they can disclose mistakes without fear of negative consequences. If students believe that their self-assessments will be inspected and judged negatively, it is logical for them to be unrealistic or dishonest in those self-assessments, which in turn will negatively influence student self-regulation and learning.

When planning and implementing self-assessment, it is easy to become focused on the technique (e.g., *We are using Traffic Lights!*) rather than on how the technique is being used to increase students' learning in relation to subject content and self-regulation. During implementation, it is important to take a step back and to reflect on how students' learning is progressing. Consideration of the following questions should help:

- What evidence do you have that students understand the purpose of the self-assessment opportunity?
- Do students appear to be conducting self-assessment in an effortful and honest way?
- What evidence is there that students are coming to understand the criteria and standards that underpin quality work?
- How do students justify the judgments they have made about their work or understanding?

Your responses to these questions should help guide their in-the-moment decisions as students participate in self-assessments. For example, you may need to make self-assessment results more or less private than originally planned. As discussed in Chapter 3, there are good reasons to let students keep self-assessments private; once an external audience is introduced, they may become less truthful. Students may worry about the teacher thinking less of them if they reveal misunderstandings, or they may display false modesty because they do not want to accidentally overestimate their abilities or performance to someone else.

However, the need for privacy must be carefully balanced with your need to understand what students think of their own work. External monitoring of self-assessment can help improve its realism because feedback can help the learner become aware of instances of overoptimism, undue pessimism, use of inappropriate criteria, or attention to less important aspects of work. Access to such data can provide you with useful insights into how students value their work and understand the criteria and standards. Although you may plan whether self-assessment will or will not be disclosed, it may be important to change those settings based on sensitivity to students' emotional signals during the activity.

Likewise, the timing and nature of self-assessment opportunities may need to change during the cycle of learning. For example, if students appear to be having trouble with a particular aspect, it may be useful to revisit the specific quality criterion in relation to that aspect. Then, students could conduct a specific self-assessment focused just on how that criterion applies to their work. However, it is important to make sure you are not expecting students to self-assess too frequently. Some students have reported boredom if self-assessment is repetitive (Ross et al., 1998). Furthermore, it is good assessment practice to not overassess, in any case.

It is also essential to have some awareness of how students are conducting their self-assessments and whether they are engaging deeply with the learning criteria and goals. There is some value in getting students to make relatively simple judgments (e.g., *This answer is correct or incorrect* or *This work is at a high or low standard in relation to criterion X*). However, we suggest that it is in the justification process that students really get a chance to develop mastery and competence in assessment of and performance in a learning domain. Although students may be able to produce accurate self-evaluations, if they do not understand or cannot articulate why their work is at a high standard, they may not be attending to appropriate features of their work. Instead, they may be basing their self-assessments on historical results (e.g., *I usually get Cs or Satisfactory on my assignments, so this one is probably a C as well*). If students do not understand why their work is a C or Satisfactory, or what qualitative differences there are between B (Good) and C (Satisfactory) levels of achievement, it is unlikely they will be able to identify the steps required to improve their work. Also, it is essential that students have the time and space to make any changes or improvements they identify.

Self-assessment opportunities may also need to be adjusted based on student affective responses both to the learning task and to the self-assessment itself. Just as it is unproductive to give students the same quiz over and over again if you know they have not yet learned the material, it is not helpful to have students repeatedly self-assess a piece of work if progress is stalled. Also, what you ask students to look for within the work may need to change based on how students are responding to the task. If students are highly motivated and progressing well, it may be fine to get them to consistently look for shortcomings and faults that can be improved within the drafting phase of a task. However, if they are finding the task very difficult, it may be helpful for motivation if they are also asked to self-assess for strengths in their work that they can build on.

Self-Reflection Phase

Although teacher monitoring and reflection should occur continuously throughout student self-assessment implementation, at the end of a cycle, there is additional deep-level reflection that can take place to inform future use of self-assessment within the classroom. It is important to gather data and identify what worked and what didn't go as planned, both for the class as a whole and for individual students. Data may come in many shapes and forms: student body language; formal evidence of achievement, such as test scores; informal conversations with students; written student comments; and so on. However, teachers need to gather data that enables them to answer important questions, including:

- Which students in the class still don't seem to fully understand the criteria and standards?
- Which students seem to understand the purpose of self-assessment and which do not?
- Were the self-assessment techniques developmentally appropriate for some or all of my students?
- Did the techniques align well with the tasks students were trying to complete?

- What challenges occurred? How were they dealt with? How can they be minimized next time?

Feedback from your own reflection on the implementation of the student self-assessment activities can help inform planning for self-assessment use within the next cycle of learning.

Just as students will often evaluate their final products with self-assessments, at the end of a cycle of learning or major task, teachers can learn a significant amount by accessing student evaluations of their work. This can be done either in conversations or via their written narrative comments. It is important to constantly look for evidence of student learning, and in this instance, it could be around content/subject matter learning or learning about self-assessment. Although teachers are used to assessing student understanding of curriculum content, student mastery of self-assessment is not usually a focus of curriculum, even though it is important to their ability to learn independently in the future. Questions teachers may want to ask after introducing self-assessment could include the following:

- Is there evidence that students are now taking more interest in the criteria and standards and actively trying to understand them?
- Have I observed students independently trying to assess their own learning against their goals or curriculum standards?
- Are students better able to name their learning processes and strategies?
- How do students now approach learning tasks? Do they seem more focused on the specific learning goals or criteria than they used to be?
- Is there evidence that students are reflecting more on their learning?

Hence, at the end of the learning cycle or task, based on the teacher's analysis of student progress in terms of learning and self-assessment, the next learning cycle or unit of work should be designed to build student competency in both of these areas.

Helping Others Implement Self-Assessment in the Classroom

Although individual teachers can implement self-assessment effectively within their own classrooms, it is ideal if an entire school (or academic department) is committed to using self-assessment as a way to help students better develop content learning and self-regulation. It may be tempting for school leaders, in light of the benefits of self-assessment, to mandate its use within a year level, department, or school. We believe that this top-down approach may be counterproductive. As shown in Chapter 3, it is very easy to implement self-assessment in naive and counterproductive ways. When poorly implemented or when sabotaged by students, self-assessment can easily turn into an exercise in deceit.

Hence, rather than adopting a top-down approach, we think it is important to approach the issue by first establishing a shared understanding of what teaching staff collectively want to achieve via self-assessment. All teachers need to understand the theory underpinning the practices and be committed to teaching self-assessment as a learned skill. Likewise, teachers likely need to be allowed some freedom to implement self-assessment in ways that will be most effective in their own classrooms given their teaching styles and the state of relationships within their classrooms. For example, if you consider Danielle's case from Chapter 3, it was clearly problematic for her to require students to disclose self-assessments, particularly in a highly public way, before trust had been established between students and their teacher and peers. Alternately, she could have allowed students to self-assess in private, engaged them in self-judgment or self-marking activities, or had them use anonymous polling software to share their self-assessments with her. Adopting strategies like these may have allowed her students to more realistically consider their own academic strengths and weaknesses.

Teachers also need to have access to quality professional development sessions or materials to help them understand and implement self-assessment. This book may be a helpful starting point, but many teachers would likely benefit from some form of peer support and interactive professional development where they can ask questions and talk specifically about their unique contexts. Interventions designed to improve teacher use of self-assessment have found models built on principles of action research to be particularly helpful (Ross et al., 1998; Wiliam, Lee, Harrison, & Black, 2004). Under such a model, teachers first learn about the practices and then develop their own action plans around how self-assessment will be integrated into their teaching. The teacher then monitors implementation, gathers data on its effectiveness, and reflects on strengths and weaknesses to create improvements in subsequent implementations. Ross et al. (1998) found a small positive effect on students' attitudes regarding self-assessment when their teachers had been introduced to it via an action research approach versus those who had learned about self-assessment via workshops more focused on the direct instruction of theories and strategies. They hypothesized that the difference may be partially because within the action research model, mentors and teachers worked together and shared control in a similar way to what needed to occur within classroom self-assessment.

It is also important that those trying to promote self-assessment implementation take teachers' concerns within their schools seriously and are willing to engage in discussions about how threats and potential problems can be dealt with within their local contexts. Ross (2006) suggests that "the number one concern of teachers about self-assessment is the fear that sharing control of assessment with students will lower standards and reward students who inflate their assessments" (p. 7). At a school level, this concern may potentially be mitigated if teachers are not expected to allow self-assessments to contribute to final grades. However, teachers may be legitimately concerned about other issues. These may include worries about parent reactions to self-assessment, fear that classroom teaching may be driven to focus on objective aspects that are easy to test and self-assess, or doubt around their own ability to manage the potential challenges arising around disclosure and student ego protection. Teachers may also doubt their students' ability or willingness to think critically about their own work. It is important to listen to teacher concerns and theories about student behavior and to work together as a team to help them see productive ways forward in relation to issues they identify; *data teams* and *learning schools* models use similar approaches when helping teachers learn to analyze and use student achievement data (Lai & Schildkamp, 2016).

It is also important to be realistic about how long it might take to see effects. Wiliam et al. (2004) noted that during their intervention designed to help teachers increase their use of formative assessment, including self-assessment, teacher behavior changed slowly. They noted that it was only toward the end of the six-month intervention that they began to really see significant changes occurring in some participants. This finding is consistent with the teacher change literature that highlights the need for sustained professional development and support (ideally across multiple years) in order to really influence practice (Timperley, Wilson, Barrar, & Fung, 2007). Indeed, research suggests that teacher professional development programs need to run from eighteen to thirty-six months in order to generate an observable effect on student learning (Brown, 2015).

Summary

In this final chapter, we have focused on how to effectively implement self-assessment in the classroom. Our recommendations are underpinned by the view that self-assessment should be a vehicle to help students learn to self-regulate (as a stand-alone and valuable skill) in addition to the benefits it may have in relation to curriculum content learning.

We recommend that teachers adopt a cycle of self-regulation, not dissimilar to what they are hoping to develop within their students. Beginning with the forethought phase, teachers must carefully select their self-assessment activities, taking into consideration system expectations, the purposes that will underpin the self-assessment activities, and students' previous experiences with and attitudes toward self-assessment. During implementation, teachers must monitor how this is progressing, taking into consideration student progress toward learning objectives and their affective reactions to self-assessment situations. Based on these data gathered in the moment, they may need to make adjustments in relation to self-assessment privacy, its timing, its frequency, or even its mode in order to help students improve desired curriculum and/or self-regulatory competence. At the conclusion of a cycle of learning or task, teachers must also engage in self-reflection, contemplating what went well and what can be further refined and improved next time.

The chapter also examined how self-assessment implementation might be guided at a school or department level. Given the challenges that can be present during implementation, as discussed in Chapter 3, we discourage a top-down approach because many forms of self-assessment will be strongly undermined if the classroom environment is not built on trust or if students do not have mind-sets that view mistakes as a normal part of learning. The first step toward systematic implementation involves helping teachers understand the theory underpinning self-assessment, but it also requires school leaders to actively listen to teacher concerns and to work together to devise strategies that mediate these in their own unique contexts. Professional development and interventions based on action research models have been found to be potentially effective and may be a good starting place. However, it is important to realize that long-term support is likely needed to see meaningful and effective change in practice. Such change requires commitment from all educational stakeholders, including students and parents.

The only way any of us can improve—as Coach Graham taught me—is if we develop a real ability to assess ourselves. If we can't accurately do that, how can we tell if we're getting better or worse?

(Pausch & Zaslow, 2008, p. 112)

References

Andrade, H. (2010). Students as the definitive source of formative assessment: Academic self-assessment and the self-regulation of learning. In H. L. Andrade & G. J. Cizek (Eds.), *Handbook of formative assessment* (pp. 90–105). New York, NY: Routledge.

Andrade, H., & Brown, G. T. L. (2016). Student self-assessment in the classroom. In G. T. L. Brown & L. R. Harris (Eds.), *Handbook of human and social conditions in assessment* (pp. 319–334). New York, NY: Routledge.

Brown, G. T. L. (2011). Self-regulation of assessment beliefs and attitudes: A review of the students' conceptions of assessment inventory. *Educational Psychology, 31*(6), 731–748. doi:10.1080/01443410.2011.599836

Brown, G. T. L. (2015). Leading school-based assessment for educational improvement: Rethinking accountability. *Rassegna Italiana di Valutazione, 19*(61), 70–81. doi:10.3280/RIV2015-061005

Brown, G. T. L., & Harris, L. R. (2013). Student self-assessment. In J. H. McMillan (Ed.), *Sage handbook of research on classroom assessment* (pp. 367–393). Thousand Oaks, CA: Sage.

Fletcher, A. K. (2016). Exceeding expectations: Scaffolding agentic engagement through assessment as learning. *Educational Research, 58*(4), 400–419. doi:10.1080/00131881.2016.1235909

Harris, L. R., & Brown, G. T. L. (2013). Opportunities and obstacles to consider when using peer- and self-assessment to improve student learning: Case studies into teachers' implementation. *Teaching and Teacher Education, 36*, 101–111. doi:10.1016/j.tate.2013.07.008

Harris, L. R., & Brown, G. T. L. (2016). Assessment and parents. In M. A. Peters (Ed.), *Encyclopedia of educational philosophy and theory* (pp. 1–6). Singapore: Springer.

Harris, L. R., Harnett, J. A., & Brown, G. T. L. (2009). "Drawing" out student conceptions: Using pupils' pictures to examine their conceptions of assessment. In D. M. McInerney, G. T. L. Brown, & G. A. D. Liem (Eds.), *Student perspectives on assessment: What students can tell us about assessment for learning* (pp. 321–330). Charlotte, NC: Information Age.

Lai, M. K., & Schildkamp, K. (2016). In-service teacher professional learning: Use of assessment in data-based decision-making. In G. T. L. Brown & L. R. Harris (Eds.), *Handbook of human and social conditions in assessment* (pp. 77–94). New York, NY: Routledge.

McMillan, J. H. (2018). *Using students' assessment mistakes and learning deficits to enhance motivation and learning.* New York, NY: Routledge.

Panadero, E., Jonsson, A., & Botella, J. (2017). Effects of self-assessment on self-regulated learning and self-efficacy: Four meta-analyses. *Educational Research Review, 22*(Supplement C), 74–98. doi:https://doi.org/10.1016/j.edurev.2017.08.004

Pausch, R., & Zaslow, J. (2008). *The last lecture*. London, England: Hodder & Stoughton.

Peterson, E. R., & Irving, S. E. (2008). Secondary school students' conceptions of assessment and feedback. *Learning and Instruction, 18*(3), 238–250.

Ross, J. A. (2006). The reliability, validity, and utility of self-assessment. *Practical Assessment, Research, and Evaluation, 11*(10), 1–13.

Ross, J. A., Rolheiser, C., & Hogaboam-Gray, A. (1998). Skills training versus action research in-service: Impact on student attitudes to self-evaluation. *Teaching and Teacher Education, 14*(5), 463–477.

Sadler, P. M., & Good, E. (2006). The impact of self- and peer-grading on student learning. *Educational Assessment, 11*(1), 1–31.

Timperley, H., Wilson, A., Barrar, H., & Fung, I. (2007). *Teacher professional learning and development (Best Evidence Synthesis Iteration (BES) report)*. Wellington, New Zealand: Ministry of Education.

Wiliam, D., Lee, C., Harrison, C., & Black, P. (2004). Teachers developing assessment for learning: Impact on student achievement. *Assessment in Education: Principles, Policy & Practice, 11*(1), 49–65. doi:10.1080/0969594042000208994

Zimmerman, B. J. (2008). Investigating self-regulation and motivation: historical background, methodological developments, and future prospects. *American Educational Research Journal, 45*(1), 166–183. doi:10.3102/00028312073

Index